Vote!: Impeach the Koch Brothers & the Do Nothing Congress.

CreateSpace Edition © Paul Covell 2014

ISBN-13: 978-1502323187

ISBN-10: 1502323184

Table of Contents

###

Senate Republicans Are Addicted to Koch.

Harry Reid

Preface

U.S. Senate Majority Leader Harry Reid (D-NV) has recognized the threat posed to the Republic by Charles Koch and David Koch, billionaire owners of Koch Industries, Inc., the second largest privately held company in the U.S, with headquarters in Wichita, Kansas. Koch campaign contributions have virtually eliminated the two party system in Kansas. From Kansas, Koch money has spread to Wisconsin to rescue Republican Governor Scott Walker from a 2012 Voter Recall. Koch Brothers want to install their own Senator in Oregon to replace Jeff Merkley. In short, the Brothers are trying to buy a Congress that will safeguard Koch Industries profits at the expense of Clean Air, Clean Water and the American consumer. As reported by *Real Clear Politics* on March 4, 2014, and captured by U-Tube, here is an excerpt from one of Senator Harry Reid's cautions about dark money—a speech on the Senate floor.

> "Charles and David Koch are shrewd businessmen. Their wealth is nearly unparalleled—not only in America, but in the world. The brothers inherited a small oil company from their dad, and built it into a multi-national corporation that refines oil, manufactures fertilizers and chemicals, makes paper products, extracts minerals, produces glass and even owns a cattle ranch.

"And like most shrewd businessmen, the oil baron Koch Brothers are very good at protecting and growing their prodigious fortune. There is nothing un-American about that.

"But what is un-American is when shadowy billionaires pour unlimited money into our democracy to rig the system to benefit themselves and the wealthiest one percent. I believe in an America where economic opportunity is open to all. But, based on their actions and the policies they promote, the Koch Brothers seem to believe in an America where the system is rigged to benefit the very wealthy.

"Based on Senate republicans' ardent defense of the Koch Brothers, and the fact that they advocate for many of the same policies the Koch Brothers do, it seems my Republican colleagues also believe in a system that benefits billionaires at the expense of the middle class. The Koch Brothers are willing to invest billions to buy that America. ***

"Koch-backed groups have spent a vast sum helping to elect Senate candidates this year—a sum that dwarfs even the National Republican Senatorial committee's own spending. The Koch Brothers and other moneyed interests are influencing the political process for their own benefit in a way not seen for generations.

"Republican Senators have come to the floor to defend the Koch Brothers' attempt to buy our democracy. Once again, Republicans are all-in to protect their billionaire friends.

"Not only have Senate Republicans come to the floor to defend the Koch Brothers personally, they have again and again defended the Koch Brothers' radical agenda. Senate Republicans have opposed closing a single tax loophole for profitable oil companies or corporations that ship jobs overseas. Senate Republicans have opposed asking billionaires to pay the same higher tax rate as middle-class families pay. Senate Republicans have opposed environmental and workplace safety standards that might cost Koch Industries or their corporate donors a few extra dollars.

"And the Koch Brothers are returning the favor with huge donations to Republican Senate candidates. Senate Republicans are addicted to Koch.***

"Senate Republicans call this freewheeling spending by anonymous donors nothing more than free speech. Senate republicans say whoever has the most money has the most free speech. But, that is not what America's Founders meant by free speech. The Founders believed in a democracy where every American has a voice and a vote.

"This discussion—this fight isn't just about health care or even a few hundred million dollars in disingenuous ads. This is about two very wealthy individuals who intend to buy their own Congress—a Congress beholden to their money and bound to enact their radical philosophy. Witness Republican Senators beholden to wealthy special interests rush to the floor to defend the Kochs whenever I say anything

negative about the brothers or their radical
agenda.***" Senator Harry Reid, March 4, 2014.

###

Koch Brothers no doubt are entitled to free
speech under the First Amendment. No one
knows what limitations, if any, an unfettered
Congress might impose on political contributions, after the Supreme Court's unlimited free
speech decisions in *Citizens United v. FEC* and
McCutcheon v. FEC. With Congress increasingly
under the influence of Koch Brothers and casino
magnate Sheldon Adelson, there is no legislative
will to address limitations on campaign financing, immigration reform, veterans care, minimum
wage, infrastructure repair or tax reform.

What is even more dangerous than unlimited
contributions to political campaigns is *dark
money* that is unidentified as to source. When
David Koch contributed to a hospital, he allowed
his name to appear on a plaque at the hospital.

When Koch Brothers use *Americans For
Prosperity*, *Freedom Partners* or *FreedomWorks*
to make anonymous contributions for political
candidates to support Koch Industries, Koch
Brothers generally hide their involvement from
the electorate. If we gut the Environmental
Protection Agency to maximize Koch Industries'
profits, it should not be in the name of freedom.
Enforcement of IRS regulations, prohibiting tax
exemption for politicking, does not offend the
First Amendment.

There *is* an IRS scandal raging. Darrell Issa,
Chair, House Committee on Oversight and
Reform, is not investigating Tea Partiers' misuse

of tax exemptions. The scandal has nothing to do with free speech. Republicans unlawfully claim tax exemption for organizations that are involved in supporting and opposing candidates for public office.

After the 2008 election, Tea Partiers submitted hundreds of applications for groups involved in politicking, but masquerading as social welfare organizations entitled to tax exemption under Internal revenue Code § 501(c)(4). Koch Brothers are also funneling money to buy Congressional seats through *Freedom Partners*, a new 501(c)(6) nonprofit, masquerading as a *Chamber of Commerce*. Koch Brothers are misusing the tax code to camouflage dark money earmarked to destroy our democratic Republic.

###

We are going to take this country back.

Raphael Cruz, Sr., immigrant from Cuba,
glad for the American Dream for his son.

Chapter 1
Hot Button Issues

Voting. Americans are passionate about their Government, but *only fifty to sixty percent* of eligible voters generally bother to vote in general elections. Voter apathy increases in mid-term elections, and frequently *only thirty-seven percent* vote when no president's name is on the ballot. Voters generally are not enthusiastic about primary elections. When the broad middle band of voters neglects their civic duty, extremists in both parties are empowered. Where

6

too many voters go to the polls angry or fanatical, or both, their delegates in Congress, being poles apart, are unable to compromise.

Gerrymander. After the 2010 census, Republicans and their Tea Party allies in nearly thirty state legislatures drew the boundaries of the election districts to give Republican and Tea Party candidates control in the U. S. House of Representatives and an increasing majority of state legislatures. Republicans' gerrymandered districts dilutes the votes of progressives.

Papers please. Republican controlled state legislatures respond to changing demographics (that would otherwise favor progressive candidates) by passing laws to tighten voter ID requirements as part of a scheme to suppress votes and intimidate voters. Our Nation is in the grip of a grassroots struggle to determine whether a *"government by the people, of the people and for the people"* can survive.

Vote. The Constitution of the United States places the power of governing in the hands of the citizens. Progressives, who sit out mid-term elections as unimportant, may find that divided government soon degrades into divisive government, and that a radical Congress may indulge the Tea Party vision of dismantling the structure of government. Tea Party zealots did not come to Washington to preach reform. *Tea Party delegates came to town figuratively to burn the Capitol down*. In the 2012 presidential primary, Governor Rick Perry (R-TX) announced his intention to close three Departments of the U.S.

Government, but, when asked at debate, Perry could not remember which three.

Minimum Wage. Federal Minimum Wage is stuck at $7.25 per hour, which does not provide a living wage. President Obama wants a minimum wage of at least $10.10 per hour, and has issued Executive Orders to require federal contractors to pay at least $10.10 per hour. If Republicans hold the House of Reprehensibles on 11/4/14, or take the Senate, Congress will not raise the Minimum Wage.

Health Care. Voter participation in mid-term elections is essential to the preservation of our Democracy. In 2010, President Obama sponsored and the Congress enacted the *Patient Protection and Affordable Care Act*. Ironically, universal health care, for forty years, was a *Republican* idea that President Richard Nixon proposed in 1973. The conservative Heritage Foundation advocated universal health care in the 1990s.

Romney Care. Governor Mitt Romney (R-MA) sponsored a mandatory state health care plan in Massachusetts in 2006. Governor Romney recommended the Massachusetts health care plan as a model for a national health care plan. MIT Professor Jonathan Gruber was a consultant on the Massachusetts plan and on the federal *Affordable Care Act*. Professor Gruber confirms that the two plans are essentially the same, and that each includes an individual mandate as envisioned by President Nixon and implemented at the state level by Governor Romney and by President Obama at the national level. According to Governor Romney, it would be unfair to allow the uninsured to resort to emergency room care that the insured inevitably pay as an increase in overall health costs.

GOP Opposition. As soon as President Obama supported a national health care plan with an individual mandate, the Republican Party turned against what essentially is a *Republican* idea. *Not one Republican* in Congress, however, voted in favor of Affordable Care for the American People. Republicans took control of the House of Representatives in 2011. From 2011-2014, Republicans in the House sponsored, debated and passed *fifty separate bills* to repeal, defund or otherwise limit or cripple the *Affordable Care Act*. The Act is not perfect, nor is it a government health insurance plan.

Standards. The Act established minimum standards for *private* health insurers to incorporate into *private* health care insurance plans. Congress should work with President Obama to improve health care and to lower costs. Affordable Care is not the only program at risk in the November 2014 election. If the Republicans and their fanatical Tea Party allies take control of the Senate, most progressive bills will be blocked, defunded or repealed.

Jobs Bill. A few years ago, (August 1, 2007) the Interstate I-35-West-Bridge collapsed and fell into the Mississippi River at Minneapolis, Minnesota. Thousands of other bridges and highways from coast to coast that have deteriorated, and America must repair the infrastructure if we are to remain competitive with China, Japan and Europe. The federal Government could and should borrow 1.7 trillion dollars *at the lowest interest rates in seventy years* to repair America's failing infrastructure. The resulting construction boom would spur employment of tens of thousands of American workers. American ingenuity, finance and hard work would finally end the Mega Recession of 2008-2009. If progressives stay home on November 4, 2014, Congress may repeal Affordable Care, and, likely, will not address immigration, jobs, minimum wage and taxation.

Nihilism. Congress does not have to impeach a president to destroy her programs. If voter apathy allows Tea Party radicals to continue to paralyze moderates, the Congress simply will repeal, defund or block most progressive programs. In 1948, President Harry Truman labeled it the *Do Nothing Congress*. Republican tactics in 1948 were the same tactics Republicans are using today. Republicans blocked the president's programs, and then complained that the president was ineffective. American voters punished the *Do Nothing* Congress in 1948, and should vote for progressive candidates and against nihilism on November 4, 2014.

Extreme Right. Today's Republicans are unable to cooperate with progressives for fear of attack by Tea Party zealots. Governor Chris Christie (R-NJ) lost standing with the right, not because of the bridge scandals, but because he was photographed walking *arm in arm* with president Obama while discussing New Jersey's share of federal relief of devastation caused by Super-Storm Sandy on October 29-31, 2012.

10

Republicans cannot agree with progressives for fear of attack from Tea Partiers and other "purists". Moderate Republicans are in peril. Senator Bob Bennett (R-UT), a conservative three term Senator, fell in the 2010 caucus and convention that favored Tea Party idol Mike Lee. Bennett aroused Tea Party ire by supporting George W. Bush's bail out of the Nation's Banking System.

No Moderates. House majority Leader Eric Cantor (R-VA) lost in the June 2014 primary to Tea Partier Dave Brat, who did not need national Tea Party assistance. Senator Thad Cochran R-MS) lost in the 2014 primary to Tea Party zealot Chris McDaniel, but, since neither won a majority, Cochran won the run-off election with the help of liberal democrats from the black community.

Miss. Yearning. McDaniel is investigating irregularities, i.e., how the less conservative candidate could win in Mississippi in an honest election. Senator Richard Lugar (R-IN), former Chair of the Foreign Relations Committee, lost the 2012 primary to more conservative Richard Mourdock, who lost to the Democrat in the general election. Lugar's offense was that he sometimes compromised with Democrats.

War. Our Nation is winding down our military occupation of Afghanistan. In 2011, U.S. combat forces withdrew from Iraq. Our previous President and by the Prime Minister of Iraq approved the 2011 withdrawal of U. S. military from Iraq. Neither President Obama, nor his predecessor was able to persuade Iraq's government to enter into a Status of Forces Agreement that would allow a residual force to remain in Iraq and give our military immunity from prosecution in Iraqi courts. After ten years of war, the American People have had enough.

Religious War. There are deep religious divisions in the Middle East. Moslems have struggled for fourteen hundred years over the succession to the Prophet. Neoconservatives and Republicans in Congress have called for, and are calling for, U.S. military intervention in Libya, Syria, Iran and Iraq, and a continued U.S. military presence in Afghanistan. However, the Congress declined to authorize military action in Syria. The Congressional authorization for use of military force in Iraq is twelve years out of date.

Iraq Government. Basher al Assad pushed rebel Islamists forces out of Syria, and the rebels now are threatening to fragment Iraq by seizing Mosul and other towns in the north and west. Sunni Kurds control Iraq's northeastern provinces. The south is the rump Iraqi Government controlled by Shia, who are under the influence of Iran. ISIL (Islamic Forces in Iraq and the Levant), also known as ISIS (Islamic Forces in Iraq and Syria) has declared a Caliphate governing Iraq, Syria and—why not—Jordan and Lebanon. President Obama initially ordered up to six hundred U. S. military to Iraq to ensure protection of American interests. However, the United States should avoid committing its military to support of one faction in a religious war in the Middle East. The U.S. cannot be the Shia Air Force.

Neocon Damage. To avoid fragmenting, Iraq must form a coalition government to include all major factions. Iraq's instability in 2014 is the result of the U.S. Invasion of 2003, the U.S. dissolution of the Sunni-led Iraqi Army, the U. S. ban on Ba'athist Party Members from government and industry positions and Prime Minister Maliki's purge of Sunni leaders after the withdrawal of U. S. military in 2011.

Jeffersonian Democracy. The United States cannot impose a Jeffersonian Democracy in Iraq by force of argument or by force of arms. Iraqis must form their own government, which will succeed or fail based upon its policy of inclusion or exclusion of representation of major factions in Iraq. Most importantly, U.S. policy makers must relegate neoconservative ambitions of Dick Cheney, Donald Rumsfeld, Paul Wolfowitz and L. Paul Bremer, to the dustbin of history, along with their Prisoner of War Camp, also known as Guantánamo.

Al-Qaeda. History will judge whether our 2003 invasion and occupation of Iraq through 2011 was justified or not. It is not helpful for President Obama to blame his predecessor for going in, or for President Bush to blame President Obama for leaving. We left because the Iraqis wanted us to leave. Some of the neoconservatives want to re-litigate the ghosts of the past.

ISIS. To those who complain of the presence of al-Qaeda or ISIS in Iraq now, they should admit that there were no al-Qaeda or ISIS in Iraq before the 2003 U. S. Invasion and eight-year occupation. Some neoconservatives see the future of U.S. foreign policy as a never-ending series of military adventures in Libya, Syria, Iraq, Iran and Afghanistan—supported by a Prisoner Of War Detention Center in Guantánamo, Cuba, that will never close because the neoconservatives do not intend the war to end—*ever*. The Nation deserves better. In Viet Nam, America was slow to realize that Vietnamese Nationalism was not necessarily a threat to the American Homeland. The grievance of al-Qaeda and bin Laden was our military presence in the Middle East.

Advice & Consent. The Congress should work with the President to determine the risk and benefit to the U. S. of any continued U. S. presence in the Middle East. U.S. Navy Seals eliminated bin Laden in May 2011, and the U. S. has disrupted al-Qaeda as a centrally controlled organization. On June 18, 2014, U. S. Special Forces and FBI Agents captured Ahmed Abu Khatallah, an alleged accomplice in the attack on the U.S. Mission at Benghazi, Libya. Mr. Khatallah will answer in U. S. District Court, and, if convicted, will serve time in the U. S. Prison System on the mainland. Guantánamo Detention Center is an aberration—and extra-legal fantasy of Dick Cheney's—that must close.

Veterans. The U. S. has more than 20 million living veterans. The Veterans Administration has seen a dramatic increase in the number of veterans seeking medical treatment since 2003. Rapid medevac procedures and equipment have saved countless lives that in former conflicts were lost on the battlefield. Saved lives means that thousands of veterans survived with serious injuries, including traumatic brain injuries caused by IEDs in Iraq and Afghanistan. VA hospitals in many states have been unable to maintain appointments in a timely manner.

VA Bonuses. The VA awarded bonuses to administrators based upon meeting or exceeding waiting times for appointments. In some cases, staff may have altered statistics on waiting times to qualify for a bonus. There will be no bonuses paid based on manipulated statistics. Violations of law go to the Justice Department for prosecution. The decision to go to war is subject to debate, but there is no question about the duty of the Nation to care for its wounded warriors. Until the VA is able to catch up on meeting goals for appointments, President Obama will seek additional funds from Congress to allow veterans to obtain treatment from doctors outside the VA's medical facilities in areas where the VA is unable to meet its appointment goals.

Investigations. Oversight is a legitimate function of Congress. Members of the House and Senate have an independent right and duty to review government programs to evaluate the use of appropriations and the execution of the law by the President. Because various programs come under the purview of more than one Committee in Congress, there may be more than one investigation of a particular matter. Since politician run for and take office, it is natural for some politics to creep into any particular Congressional Investigation. The value of any Congressional Investigation, however, is inversely proportional to the level of politics involved. When an Investigation is purely for political purposes, there is virtually no oversight value. Aside from their fixation on destroying health care for the American People, today's Congress (when in session) wastes time with politicized investigations.

Tax Exemption. President Obama's election in 2009 spawned hundreds of newly formed organizations, including many with the name Tea Party, that applied for tax exempt status under Internal Revenue Code § 501(c)(4). The law, as written, allowed tax exempt status if the mission statement of the applicant *exclusively* was for social welfare as opposed to supporting or opposing the candidacy of a particular office seeker or office holder.

Social Welfare. In 1969, the IRS issued an extra-legal ruling that an applicant could be granted tax-exempt status if the mission statement covers *primarily* social welfare. The law and the IRS Ruling inevitably caused the IRS to investigate the proposed activity of applicants for tax-exempt status to determine whether the proposed activity was primarily for social welfare purposes. If the Congress wants to change the law, and have another agency, say the Federal Election Commission, review the mission statement of social welfare groups to determine eligibility for tax exemption, the President likely will cooperate in making such change.

IRS Commissioner. John Koskinen became IRS Commissioner in January 2014. Mr. Koskinen has more than twenty-five years of honorable service in government and in private business. As IRS Commissioner, Mr. Koskinen spends much of his time responding to *five* different Congressional Investigations into IRS review of applicants for tax exempt status for 501(c)(4) groups.

Search Term. Because there were more than a thousand of applications pending for tax-exempt status in 2010 and 2011, well before Mr. Koskinen's appointment, the IRS improperly used the term *"Tea Party"* as a search term and short cut to identify each organization that *might be involved* in political activities in support or opposition to an office seeker or office holder.

I.G. As the law is written and applied, the IRS is required to investigate the activities of each social welfare organization that seeks tax exempt status. The Inspector General of the Treasury Department found the use of the term "Tea Party" as a short cut, search term, improper, and the IRS stopped using "Tea Party" as a search term.

Disrespect. Because criticism of the IRS is popular with the Tea Party, many Republican Members of Congress have gone out of their way to disrespect the IRS Commissioner during his many hours of testimony on IRS procedures in use to grant tax exempt status *before* Mr. Koskinen's appointment as IRS Commissioner. Chairman Darrell Issa's Government Oversight Committee has shown such disrespect for the IRS Commissioner that Ranking Member Elijah Cummings and other Democrats have apologized to Mr. Koskinen on the record. Trey Gowdy (R-SC) (chosen to chair the Select Committee on Benghazi) virtually accused the IRS and its

Commissioner of spoliation of evidence without any proof.

Conspiracy. The Republicans have concluded, without any proof, that there was a conspiracy between Lois Lerner, the IRS Official charged with supervision of processing applications for tax exempt status, and the IRS in Washington, or the White House, or both. President Obama, according to nihilists, used the IRS to punish Tea Party critics of the Obama administration and to counter the removal of limits on campaign contributions decided in *Citizens United v. Federal Election Commission*.

Lois Lerner. The Republicans have conjured up a conspiracy based upon Lois Lerner's loss of some of her e-mail IRS communications after crash of a hard disk drive. Republicans complain that the IRS is violating Tea Party Group's First Amendment rights of political expression. Tea Party Groups, however, are free to criticize whomever they choose. The law requires the IRS to determine whether a group is entitled to tax-exempt status so long as its activities are primarily for social welfare purposes. There is no evidence of a conspiracy, and there is no evidence that the IRS denied tax-exempt status to silence any group, including any Tea Party Group.

Exemption Generally Granted. After a review of political activities, *which is mandated by Internal Revenue Code § 501(c)(4)*, virtually all applicants have been granted tax exempt status. Doubtless, Congress should revise and clarify the law, and, perhaps, designate another less intrusive Agency to review applications. Republicans, however, do not want to cooperate to replace the confused status quo with a revised law and process that might be workable. Nihilists are quite content to maintain the tangled status of the law and application process to continue the attack on government. Darrell Issa (R-CA), Chairman of the House Government Oversight Committee is using the investigation to convict Lois Lerner (before any trial and before any formal accusation) and to disrespect IRS Commissioner Koskinen—who took office in January 2014—three or four years after the events of which nihilists complain.

Benghazi. Republicans appointed Trey Gowdy Chairman of a Select Committee to investigate the attack on our consulate in Benghazi, Libya, on September 11, 2012, when Islamist terrorists murdered Ambassador Chris Stevens and three other consular officials. Chairman Gowdy, a former federal and local prosecutor, has already remarked that he will conduct the hearing as a trial. The presumption is that there will be a show trial to discourage former Secretary of State Hillary Clinton from running for President in 2016, or to inflict mortal wounds if she does decide to run.

Witch Hunt. There have already been multiple investigations of the Benghazi attack, including a nonpartisan investigation by the State Department. If Chairman Gowdy indulges the Tea Party radicals, he will allow the Select Committee on Benghazi to become a witch-hunt. The Select Committee may want to review what effect there was on the safety of the Benghazi Diplomatic Mission by Congress cutting three hundred million dollars from the State Department security budget for 2011.

Legacy. If there is any legacy intact at the end of President Obama's second term, it will not be for the President. It will be for the American People. At the urging of the Tea Party, Republicans determined to block all progressive initiatives of the Obama Administration. *While the President was trying to waltz with Michelle at the Inaugural Balls on January 20, 2009, six hours after taking the oath of office, Congressional Republicans were meeting just down the street to agree—conspire, if you will— to block all things Obama.* Impeachment is the least of the President's concerns.

GOP Plan. What is truly frightening is that, if the Republicans maintain control of the House and take control of the Senate on November 4, 2014, the Tea Party will begin its attack on government itself. The nihilists will repeal the *Affordable Care Act*, give low dollar vouchers for Medicare and Medicaid, and privatize Social Security. Nihilists will appropriate ample funds, however, for John McCain and neoconservatives to *"bomb, bomb, bomb"* Iran, Iraq and Syria.

Immigration. On June 27, 2013, the U.S. Senate passed a comprehensive immigration bill by a vote of 68-32. Things rapidly went downhill from there. Speaker John Boehner (R-OH) initially announced that the House would take up its own immigration bill, but decided in 2014 that the house was too busy (not in the Capitol enough days) to consider immigration. Senator Marco Rubio (R-FL) was an eager co-sponsor of the 2013 Senate Immigration Bill. Rubio was counting on a few million sympathetic Hispanic votes he might win nationally in a 2016 presidential bid based on immigration reform that included a path to citizenship for undocumented workers.

Rubio Walks. Rubio later denounced his own immigration bill when he realized that supporting a path to citizenship for undocumented workers likely would cost him the Republican Party Nomination, and, if nominated, would cost upwards of twenty million votes of Tea Party zealots and others opposed to a path to citizenship for the undocumented. Rubio turned against the history of his own parents, whom Congress granted American citizenship, albeit his parents emigrated as *economic* refugees from Cuba in 1956, with visas, before the rise of Fidel Castro. If Marco Rubio's parents were Cubans today, they would not qualify for U. S. visas in the present toxic mood against immigration.

Cruz Control. If Raphael Cruz, Sr., firebrand father of Tea Party darling, Senator Raphael (Ted) Cruz, Jr, (R-TX), were Cuban today, the U.S. would not admit him as it did in 1957 on a student visa to study at the University of Texas. For a Nation of Immigrants, it is ironic that the political offspring of immigrants want to block the path and door to citizenship enjoyed by their parents, and in some cases, grandparents.

Impeachment. Dynamics for the U.S. House to impeach President Obama are moving inexorably ahead. Critics in the Republican Clown Car: Dick Cheney, Sarah Palin, Donald Trump, Rush Limbaugh, Sean Hannity, John McCain, Lindsey Graham, Kelly Ayotte, Bobby Jindal, Rick Perry, Scott Walker, Michele Bachmann, Marco Rubio and Marsha Blackburn, blame President Obama for all evils, foreign and domestic. Tea Party radicals, led by Chief Clown Donald Trump, refused to acknowledge President Obama's U. S. citizenship. If the dreaded House Un-American Affairs Committee (HUAC) of the 1950s were extant, some nihilist like Darrell Issa would call the President to account for having a Kenyan father. Republicans in Congress decided on Inauguration Day that they would oppose the President's policies. Upon taking control of the House in 2011, nihilists shut the government down figuratively in general and literally in October 2013 rather than work with the President on a budget. Nihilists accuse the President of imperialism, doing too much on his own, and inattentiveness, doing too little.

Boehner's Lawsuit. In June 2014, Speaker Boehner announced a lawsuit by the House to compel the President to enforce the Affordable Care Act. The President delayed the employer mandate for one year, which Republicans wanted to do with the mandate and with the entire law. The Courts will be perplexed with a lawsuit where the plaintiffs have suffered no injury and the President did what the Congress wanted done.

Practice Impeachment. Tea Partiers see the lawsuit as a warm-up to Impeachment. Boehner is aghast that Democrats are using the lawsuit and the threat of Impeachment to raise campaign contributions. On July 30, 2014, House Republicans voted to sue President Obama for acting on his own. On July 31, Boehner withdrew a $169 million border control measure that was destined to fail when Senator Ted Cruz whipped Tea Party House Members against it. A day after suing President Obama for using Executive Orders to solve problems, Boehner excused the failure of the meager border control measure by noting that there are measures the President can take by himself to address problems, without Congressional action.

Do Something. President Obama responded to the House lawsuit by urging the House to take up necessary legislation, for example, the Immigration Bill passed by the Senate in June 2013. The House is too busy (not in the Capitol enough days) to vote on immigration reform, despite the fact that up to nine thousand unaccompanied children from Central America are arriving at the U.S.-Mexico border some months. U.S. immigration law complicates the problem.

Central America. Children who cross the U.S. border as nationals from Canada or Mexico generally go back immediately. Children who cross the U.S. border as nationals from other countries, including Central America, must go into custody. Department of Health and Human Services must protect them. Immigration must give them a hearing, which can take two years.

Impeach Whom. President Obama announced that he address immigration by executive order, in the face of House obstruction. It is a virtual certainty that someone will be impeached. Either Tea Party radicals in the House will impeach President Obama by February 13, 2015, or the voters will impeach and oust the nihilists at the polls on November 4, 2011. Status quo paralysis in Congress is unsustainable.

Bar None. Former Rep Bob Barr (R-GA) is in between jobs, and looking to re-renter the political field. Not surprisingly, Barr is on the impeachment bandwagon along with such luminaries as Sarah Palin, Louie Gohmert (R-TX), Jason Chaffetz (R-UT) and Michele Bachmann (R-MN). Barr introduced the first bill to impeach President Clinton in 1997, *before* impeaching Clinton became fashionable. Barr's claim to fame in 2014 is no different. Barr dusted off the Clinton Impeachment Articles, changed a few words, and thought it sounded a lot like Articles of Impeachment for President Obama. Barr is most unremembered for his eminently forgettable book—*The Meaning of Is: The Squandered Impeachment and Wasted Legacy of William Jefferson Clinton*. Barr ran for President in 2008 as a Libertarian, and was barred from the Obama-McCain debates. In 2012, Barr supported Newt Gingrich over Ron Paul. Barr claimed the GOP left him, believes in Big Government and encroaches on civil liberties through NSA intercepts of e-mail and telephone communi-cations. Barr returned to the Republican Party and unsuccessfully ran for Congress in 2012 and 2014.

11/4/14. It is important for the American People to vote on November 4, 2014. There is no president's name on the ballot. The president's policies, however, will succeed or fail depending on whom the people send to Congress. There is no war or peace referendum on the November Ballot. There is no referendum on the Ballot on Affordable Care or Infrastructure Repair. If the Tea Party continues to take over the Congress, however, social programs and jobs bills likely will yield to military adventures and an attack on government itself. The penalty for voter apathy is unresponsive government.

2016, Too Late. No one should wait until the presidential election in November 2016 to vote in the more important election. By then, it may be too late. The mid-term election of 2010, which some progressives sat out, was vitally important because it allowed Republicans to draw gerrymandered districts that ensured Republican control of the U. S. House and in an increasing majority of state legislatures. The mid-term election of 2014 is vitally important to elect a Congress that will work with the Executive for the benefit of the American People. "Do-Nothing" and "Obstructionism" are not part of a legislative plan. They are slogans used by nihilists to attack Government itself. House Speaker John Boehner claims credit, not for bills passed, but for bills blocked. If the House will not consider bills, such as the Immigration Bill passed by the senate in June 2013, why come to town? The House calendar shows a preference for increased absence from the Capitol.

Vote by Mail. Most of the hysteria about voter ID would melt away, if the entire vote is by mail. In-person vote-fraud is rare. Voter fraud generally involves absentee ballots or writing in names by election officials. Therefore, at first blush, it seems counterintuitive to suggest conducting the entire vote by mail. However, that is exactly what the State of Oregon has done. *There are no polling places in Oregon to accommodate in-person voting.* Everyone in Oregon votes by mail. There are no reports of widespread voting fraud in Oregon. It seems that in other states, where absentee ballots comprise only fifteen to twenty percent of the vote, there is a temptation to use absentee ballots to distort the outcome of the vote. Voting fraud may be less when the entire vote is by mail. Nihilists may oppose having elections by mail, because that would tend to increase the turnout. Voters who do not want to wait in line for four hours would find it more convenient to vote by mail.

Turnout. Republicans know from experience that large voter turnout generally gives Democrats a better chance to win. Not wanting to lose their newfound power, Republicans are keeping their *thumb on the scale* to make sure the Democratic masses do not have all of their votes counted. Following the election of Barack Obama to the White House, thirty legislatures saw fraudulent voting as the number one evil to address.

Vote Suppression. The answer was stricter voter ID laws, which allow states to control who can vote. Republicans use vote suppression and voter intimidation to keep out progressives. Stricter voter ID laws was a reaction to the election of the first black President in 2008 and the announcement by the Census Bureau that after 2011 the majority of babies born in the U.S. would be born into minority families.

Forecast. The mid-term election of November 4, 2014, is easy to predict. If voter turnout is 37 percent or less, Republicans will increase their hold on the House and, likely take control of the Senate. If voter turnout is 60 percent or more (suggesting that the American People have had enough of *Koch Brothers' Nihilist Congress of 2011-2015*), Democrats may take back the House and hold the Senate.

Resources. If enough voters in Miami-Dade County and other high population centers have to wait in line for more than four hours to vote, Republican Governor Rick Scott may be re-elected. The sad truth is that Republican Governors can affect election results by limiting resources available to Democratic leaning precincts. By holding down availability of voting machines in progressive precincts, Republicans can give an unfair advantage to Republican candidates. If the masses of voters can vote, Democrats have a better chance to prevail. Governor Scott knows that it takes a long time to vote in the most progressive precincts of Miami-Dade County. We will see what, if anything, Governor Rick Scott and Secretary of the State of Florida, Ken Detzner, do to help Floridians vote without waiting in long lines for hours.

Supreme Court. If progressives are happy with Supreme Court decisions in *Burwell v. Hobby Lobby*, *Citizens United v. Federal Election Commission* and *McCutcheon v. Federal Election Commission*, then just sit out the mid-term election on November 4, 2014. Real Clear Politics estimates that Republicans will take control of the Senate 51 to 49, after picking up Alaska, Arkansas, Louisiana, Montana, South Dakota and West Virginia. Once the Senate is in control of nihilists, confirmation of progressive nominees to any federal court will be difficult.

##

*By the autumn of 1953, Washington was
a city in the grip of a witch-hunt.*

American Prometheus, the Triumph & Tragedy of J. Robert Oppenheimer, Vintage Books, 2006, softcover, p. 478

Chapter 2
Benghazi, Benghazi, Bergdahl?!

Many things have changed in Washington, D. C., and in the Halls of Congress since the witch hunts of the 1950s. Names of accusers and targets are different. Character assassination and the base art of the smear today, however, use the same methods honed by the late Senator Joseph McCarthy (R-WI). Then, the magic words were *Communism, Loyalty* and *Security*. Today, the buzz words are *Security, Terrorism* and *American Exceptionalism*.

McCarthy was too volatile to trust in the high-tech lynching of J. Robert Oppenheimer. Lewis Strauss, Chair of the infant Atomic Energy

Commission, personally urged FBI Director Hoover and President Eisenhower that Oppenheimer's Security clearance should revoke so a less gifted Strauss could shine brighter.

Today, in the eyes of the Tea Party, the enemy is the government itself. The nihilists agreed—conspired, if you will—on Inauguration Day 2009, that they would unite in Congress to deprive President Obama of any legislative achievement. Fully expecting to block all initiatives, nihilists planned to condemn Obama as incompetent, or, even worse, un-American. Nihilists and war hawks would complain that Obama was soft on terrorism and unwilling to flex America's military muscle in Libya, Syria, Iraq and Afghanistan. One signature bill survived nihilist' obstruction. *The Affordable Care Act* became law in 2010, without one Republican vote, while progressives controlled both House and Senate.

Frustrated by their inability to dismantle healthcare from 2011-2014, the nihilists desperately searched for another *cause célèbre*. Her name is Hillary. Nothing personal. Hillary Clinton, however, would be a formidable candidate, if she chooses to run for president in 2016.

A good, old-fashioned, witch hunt just might influence Hillary not to run. Benghazi offers a bonus. Attack President Obama and Hillary at the same time. Hillary was Secretary of State on September 11, 2012, when Islamic militants attacked the American Diplomatic Mission at Benghazi, Libya, and murdered U. S. Ambassador

Chris Stevens and three other consular officers. Nihilists are determined to drag the memory of *Four Dead Americans* through a mock trial staged mainly to convince Hillary Clinton not to run for president.

It is an open secret that the CIA operated the Benghazi Diplomatic Mission. The State Department and Hillary Clinton did not control the Benghazi facility. CIA involvement complicated the particulars and the tone of the explanation that the U.S. would give concerning the sack of the Benghazi Consulate. Susan Rice, Ambassador to the U.N., appeared on the Sunday Talk Shows to explain the tragedy.

CIA censors fashioned *Talking Points* for Rice to follow. The Company Line was that the Benghazi incident was merely a spillover from the riots that broke out in Cairo earlier the same day, following publicity about an anti-Moslem video made by an agitator in California months before. Susan Rice followed the CIA script. Rice failed to assert or conjecture that Benghazi was a planned terrorist attack carried out by Islamists allied with al Qaeda.

This slip-up and the firestorm generated in nihilists' ranks later would cause Susan Rice to withdraw her name for consideration as Secretary of State to replace Hillary Clinton. Rice's other fatal flaw in nihilist terms was her statement two years later that Bowe Bergdahl, who the U. S. swapped for five top Taliban prisoners, had served the U. S. Army *honorably and with distinction*. It appeared that Bergdahl walked off his post in Afghanistan in an unauthorized absence. Nihilists want to attack Bergdahl and Susan Rice as convenient surrogates for continuing the war of words against President Obama.

As time passed, nihilists feared that Hillary would run for president. Benghazi might serve to cut short another career. Nihilists already investigated Benghazi a number of times. Darrell Issa (R-CA) made a mockery of legislative investigation in the House Oversight and Government Reform Committee. Howard P. ("Buck") McKeon (R-CA), Chair of the House Armed Services Committee, had a go at politicizing Benghazi. Congress held hearings in five other investigations of Benghazi. State Department officials conducted a nonpartisan investigation.

There will always be more details to be uncovered, but the basic facts surrounding the Benghazi attack are fully explored and defined. One fact ignored was that nihilists in the House cut $330 million from the State Department Security Budget for 2011. The physical facility of the Benghazi Mission and Annex was nothing more than a few unprotected villas in two locations, open to attack by anyone with a pick-up truck, an AK-47 and a few Rocket Propelled Grenades.

Despite all of the previous hearings and investigations of Benghazi, the exigency of the political situation in 2014 spurred the House nihilists to empower a Select Committee to conduct a smear Hillary, super hearing on

Benghazi. The exigency was that Hillary might run and likely would win the presidency in 2016.

Rallying causes for nihilists were scarce. After fifty futile House bills failed to bring down *Affordable Care*, and after more than ten million people signed up for health insurance by 2014, nihilist troops were desperate for a new banner to inspire the base. Nihilist hysteria over the IRS investigations of Internal Revenue Code §501(c)(4) organizations seeking tax exemption failed to ignite public support.

The law was clear. Tax exemption was valid only if the organization was engaged *exclusively* in social welfare, with no politicking permitted. In 1969, the IRS mindlessly gutted the efficacy of the law with an extra-legal regulation that allowed politicking, if the organization was engaged *primarily* in social welfare. That ruling hopelessly blurred the line between what a 501(c)(4) organization could and could not do, and maintain tax exempt status. In confusing the law, the IRS bought itself the political nightmare of investigating the activities of each political organization that applied for 501(c)(4) tax exemption. IRS investigation of political groups, to verify tax-exempt status, was not a rallying cry against the federal government until 2009.

Barack Obama's election in 2008 spurred an avalanche of Tea Party groups who were trying to square the circle. Tea Party groups from coast to coast wanted tax exempt status under 501(c)(4) to politick against the President. From 2009 to 2012, the IRS tried to do its job, under the bizarre 1969 interpretation of 501(c)(4), by investigating the extent of the political activities of the Tea Party groups to assess qualification for tax exempt status. Tea Party groups screamed foul, and nihilists on Capitol Hill called for investigations. Public outcry did not materialize, and Hillary presented a more enticing target for a witch hunt.

Ironically, the chaos in Tripoli, *two years after* the Benghazi attack, resulted in the U.S. Embassy closing and removing staff from Libya.at the end of July 2014. This is probably what the U.S. should have done in 2012 at Benghazi before the attack. Nihilists will criticize America's withdrawal.

The truth of the matter, however, is that host countries must provide protection for U. S. Embassies and Consulates. U.S. diplomats should not be in danger in chaotic conditions. Nor can the U.S. military act as sheriff for countries whose governments are disintegrating. Neocon-servatives, led by Dick Cheney and John McCain are wrong. The people of Libya and Iraq should sort out what type of government they should have. Dick Cheney's 2003 invasion of Iraq served only to fragment the Iraq Government and increase the power of Iran in the region. Another surge in military force will not end the chaos.

L Paul Bremer became Administrator of the Iraq *Coalition Provisional Authority* on May 12, 2003. Bremer carried out the orders of Cheney and Paul Wolfowitz, dismantled the Iraqi Army (making thousands of officers vulnerable to insurgency), prohibited three levels of Ba'athist Party Members from positions in Government and

Industry, caused an Insurgency and fragmenting of Iraq—and, after destroying Iraq—boarded a plane and flew home a year later. Mission Accomplished. Iraq as a viable nation was finished. Blame Obama.

A Benghazi show-trial to bring down Hillary was something the frenzied Republican, nihilist base could sink their teeth into. The American People just might join the fray, as a bonus, *if nihilists properly invoked patriotism.* Member after member of the nihilists in the House and Senate bowed their heads and solemnly invoked the memory and incanted the mantra of *Four Dead Americans* to justify a witch hunt to smear Hillary Clinton.

It was time to finish off Hillary before she could announce her candidacy. Nihilists trotted out their super star: Representative Trey Gowdy (R-SC), a former federal and local prosecutor from Spartanburg, South Carolina. Born Harold Watson Gowdy III, Trey soon let it slip that he would conduct the Benghazi hearing as a trial. Some of the families of the *Four Dead Americans* were aghast about the politicization of the tragedy.

Progressives at first considered boycotting the Panel because there was concern that the nihilists would abuse their power of the gavel. After consulting her Conference, Nancy Pelosi (D-CA), Minority Leader, announced that the Democrats would participate to try to keep the nihilists honest. Elijah Cummings (D-MD), who exposed the abuses of Darrell Issa (R-CA), Chair of the House IRS Tax Exempt Organization investigation, will be ranking member for the progressives in the Benghazi witch hunt.

Trey Gowdy is a member of Darrell Issa's Government Oversight Committee that held an unusual evening hearing on June 23, 2014. It was time to savage IRS Commissioner John Koskinen one more time. Gowdy snarled at Koskinen that spoliation of evidence would permit a jury to draw a negative inference. Koskinen allowed that he was not sure what Gowdy was saying. The disrespect by Issa and the nihilists toward Koskinen was such an embarrassment that most of the progressives on the panel apologized for the behavior of the nihilists.

Issa quickly admonished the Democrats that House Rules forbade questioning the motives of other panel members. Issa's admonishment was a tacit admission that the Committee was involved in a witch hunt to smear President Obama and IRS Commissioner Koskinen, who had been in office only since January 2014. Nihilist members repeatedly asked Koskinen why he did not tell them in March 2014, that some of Lois Lerner's e-mails could not be recovered. Koskinen explained that he was not aware of the missing e-mails until later. Nihilists were hysterical in demanding to know why the IRS did not inform Congress sooner. No one asked the nihilists the pointed question. *What would they have done differently had they known in March that certain Lois Lerner e-mails were not recoverable?*

Issa and the nihilists frequently implied that the President, through the IRS, was depriving the Administration's political opponents of free speech guaranteed by the First Amendment. This is a total mischaracterization of the issue. The issue is qualification for tax exemption, not free speech. *Members of Tea Parties and their political organizations are free to criticize any one they choose.* The law instructs the IRS to grant tax exempt status to organizations formed exclusively for purposes of social welfare. Internal Revenue Code §501(c)(4).

An extra-legal interpretation of the law by the IRS in 1969 provided for tax exemption if the purpose of the organization was *primarily* for social welfare. The procedure required the organization to apply for tax status, and required the IRS to review the organization's activities to determine if the activities were *primarily* for social welfare.

Ironically, nihilists have been unable to identify one 501(c)(4) organization that was denied tax exempt status for advocating against President Obama. Ultimately, the IRS granted tax exempt status to virtually all applicants. Congress should simplify the process by enacting a replacement law that makes sense and takes the IRS out of reviewing political activities. The Congressional investigations of IRS processing 501(c)(4) applicants were and are a tempest in a teapot.

Another dodge nihilists are using is to hide dark money in a tax exempt 501(c)(6) organization, such as *Freedom Partners*, a Virginia group used by the Koch Brothers to funnel money to other right wing groups. According to the IRS, 501(c)(6) tax exempt status would be appropriate for Business leagues, Chambers of Commerce, Real Estate Boards and Professional football leagues.

Freedom Partners' objective of buying a Congress for the Koch Brothers does not fit any legitimate category of 501(c)(6) organizations. Nihilists are taking advantage of the brouhaha—resulting from the House investigation of the IRS—to set up illegal tax exempt organizations.

Freedom Partners was set up as a 501(c)(6) faux *Chamber of Commerce* because the reporting is less burdensome than for a 501(c)(4) organization. The IRS should cancel tax exemption of *Freedom Partners* for misleading about the mission statement of the organization.

Modern witch hunts do *not* want to catch a witch. The object of a witch hunt is to smear the quarry's reputation, to assassinate their character and to slander their name to accomplish an unsavory political goal. The innocent women hanged in Salem, Massachusetts, in the 1690s were sacrificial pawns in the convulsions of the church-state theocracy, and suffered a fate similar to the victims at the hands of modern day Islamists in Iran, Iraq and Syria.

Republican witch hunts frequently evolve at a leisurely pace. Ongoing smear from a continuing show trial is the payoff. When asked about the timing of the hearings anticipated by the Select Committee on Benghazi, House Speaker John Boehner (R-OH) explained on 5/22/14 that it would take considerable time to review the record developed at the other hearings before the Select Committee could start its production.

Boehner could not disclose the truth. The nihilists (whenever they *visit* the Capitol in between breaks) would like to present some drama in the summer and fall of 2014 to influence the November mid-term election, and have a curtain call in 2015 and beyond to motivate the base for the general election in 2016. If the Benghazi witch hunt had no legitimate purpose, there was no rush to begin or to conclude the charade by any date certain.

Holding sessions only fifty percent of the time made it difficult for the Republican House to accomplish its objectives. Progressives wanted an even number from each side on the Select Committee to insure nonpartisan proceedings. Nihilists refused to grant equality of vote or to give equal voice in issuing subpoenas or screening witnesses. The sole purpose of the Select Committee on Benghazi was to derail the presidential chances of Hillary Clinton. Fairness was not a consideration. The families of the *Four Dead Americans* could only look on in shock as the nihilists made a mockery of the deaths of their loved ones.

What Difference, At This Point, Does It Make?
Hillary made this response to Senator Ron Johnson (R-WI) at the Senate Foreign Relations Committee Hearing on January 23, 2013, questioning whether the Benghazi attack was planned, pre-planned, al Qaeda-related, spontan-eous, or merely a demonstration over the Moslem-baiting video that spurred riots in Cairo earlier on the day of the attack.

Nihilists will play Hillary's response to the gallery for political effect, coupled with a byline referring to *Four Dead Americans*. Hillary's point, however, was to honor the sacrifice of her friend, Ambassador Chris Stevens, and the other three murdered Americans, to stop the rhetoric and to appropriate sufficient funds to make U. S. Diplomatic Missions safe.

What the Select Committee will never do is admit that it is virtually impossible to protect all of our Diplomatic Missions all the time. Primary responsibility for perimeter protection of embassies and consulates lies with the host country.

In 2011, Libya was chaotic and in the throes of a civil war that ended forty years of dictatorship by Muammar Gaddafi. Unlike Iraq, which had some government infrastructure to replace its dictator, Libya was a one-man show. Without the strong man, Libya descended into chaos and civil war. By 2014, what was left of Iraq's government structure disintegrated in a Civil War between Sunni and Shiite Moslems.

The fledgling replacement Libyan Government in 2011 had no institutions to hold the country together. Armed militias roamed the streets. Ambassador Stevens could have secluded himself in the relatively safer U. S. Embassy in Tripoli. Benghazi, in eastern Libya, was one of the first areas to fall to the rebels in the uprising against Gaddafi. However, there were still dangerous elements in Benghazi who were hostile to the U.S.

Ambassador Stevens put himself in harm's way purposely because he believed in the revolution that toppled Gaddafi. He believed that he could help secure and shape a democratic Libya, allied with America in reforming the Middle East.

In contrast to the high ideals of Ambassador Stevens, the House Select Committee intends to make a mockery of *Four Dead Americans* in a witch-hunt calculated *to ward off the presidential candidacy of Hillary Clinton*. By staging a show trial, nihilists admit that they do not have a contender who could beat Hillary Clinton in 2016.

Dissing Bowe Bergdahl's Dad

Nihilists hit a new low by celebrating and quickly retreating from President Obama's announcement on 5/31/14 of the exchange of U.S. Army Sergeant Bowe Bergdahl for five top Taliban leaders. Since any friend of President Obama is the nihilists' enemy, the ferocious turn against Sergeant Bergdahl included attacking his dad. Why did the father grow a beard to become a Taliban look-alike? Why, the father even learned Pashto to be able to communicate with the Taliban?!

Kudos to Chuck Todd, on *Morning Joe*, CNBC, June 5, 2014, from Normandy, France, for warning a querulous Joe Scarborough away from attacking Bergdahl's father for trying to get his son released. Senator John McCain appears to be playing politics by acting as if the Bergdahl-Taliban exchange were unexpected. McCain forgot about his taped interview with Anderson

Cooper in February 2014. McCain described the possibility of a Bergdahl-Taliban exchange.

McCain thought the exchange would be a good idea in February 2014. As soon as President Obama ordered the exchange three months later, McCain turned tail. Exchanging the hardest of the hardcore Taliban leaders is too dangerous, according to McCain. Faced with his February interview on CNN, McCain will have to retreat to raising questions about the details of the exchange. Even Diane Feinstein (D-CA), Chair, Senate Intelligence Committee, complained about the President's failure to give thirty days' notice of the exchange of five Taliban leaders for Bergdahl.

Tres Caballeros Andantes

Senator McCain frequently appears on camera with Senators Lindsey Graham (R-SC) and Kelly Ayotte (R-NH), speaking with a unitary voice against their President. Once in front of a camera, the three nihilist Caballeros invariably launch a joint attack on President Obama.

Let's unpack the motivations of the *Tres Caballeros Andantes.* McCain never got over his 2008 loss to Obama. For McCain, it was a humiliating defeat. McCain could not understand how the Nation could choose a *Johnny-Come-Lately* over a seasoned veteran.

McCain served in Congress since 1982. Obama served seven years in the Illinois Senate and two years in the U.S. Senate. McCain served in Viet Nam as a Naval Aviator, was shot down, imprisoned five years and tortured. Obama never served in the military.

McCain is gentleman enough not to try to blame Sara Palin for his 2008 loss to Obama-Biden. McCain never forgave Obama. McCain was re-elected handily to the Senate in 2012, so he does not have to fear imminent Tea Party challenge. At all events, McCain rejects most of what Obama does or proposes. McCain gave up his role as a voice of moderation to take on the sterile character of a sore loser.

Lindsey Graham was afraid the Tea Party might push him out office in the June 2014, South Carolina, primary, which Graham won. In his criticism of President Obama, Lindsey was just trying to look tough and as far right as possible. Lindsey Graham cannot afford to look like a wimp, after election to strongman Strom Thurmond's seat in the Senate. Without Tea Party threats from the right, Graham would be a voice of moderation. To placate the extremists, Graham had to abandon his former compromise approach to immigration and climate change.

Kelly Ayotte has Tea Party support, which she is desperately trying to hold onto by criticizing all things Obama. Ayotte has the same problem that McCain has, being on both sides of the Bergdahl-Taliban prisoner swap. Ayotte sent a tweet on May 22nd, 2014, urging the Department of Defense to do what it takes to bring Bowe Bergdahl home.

Although Bergdahl, a native of Idaho, has no connection with New Hampshire, Senator Ayotte wrote numerous letters to Defense Secretaries Leon Panetta and Chuck Hagel, ultimately asking the DoD *to redouble its efforts to find Sergeant*

Bergdahl and return him safely to his family. As soon as President Obama announced Bowe Bergdahl's release, Ayotte saw only the danger in releasing five top Taliban from Guantánamo.

What the nihilists fail to see is that the prisoner exchange is the beginning of Obama's bold initiative and opening to the Taliban, symbolized by the winding down of the war and presaged by release of five top Taliban leaders. Obama's initiative may fail, and likely will fail, but it was necessary.

There is no precedent and no justification to keep prisoners of war forever. Any prisoner, who is not charged, tried and convicted of war crimes, must go free at the end of the war. Nihilists want perpetual war, perpetual U.S. military presence in Afghanistan and Iraq, and perpetual detention of jihadists in Guantánamo. The American People elected and re-elected President Obama to end the wars and to bring American troops home from Iraq and Afghanistan.

Why should the U.S. acquiesce in the nihilist's default policy that America should continue to be at war with Moslem fundamentalists forever? The devil may be in the details or may be in the politics of destruction. The *Three Caballeros Andante* and their nihilist allies are poisoning the well from which all Americans must eventually drink.

The fact that ISIS (Islamic State in Iraq and Syria), a group that al-Qaeda rejects as too violent, took over the northern Iraq City of Mosul and is threatening Baghdad and Irbil, does not mean that the U. S. will or should send ground troops back to Iraq. Senator John McCain continues his ten-year rant that the U. S. must become more involved militarily in Iraq, Libya, Syria, Afghanistan and Iran. McCain is a former fighter pilot, who flies by the seat of his pants. The American people elected and re-elected President Obama to end wars, not to jump into every fray that presents itself.

Benghazi Stand Down Order Debunked

Chairman Issa and far right allies, such as Jason Chaffetz (R-UT), have conjured up a conspiracy theory to prove that Hillary Clinton is not worthy of becoming president. Nihilists allege that Hillary gave an order for the military team in Tripoli, Libya (which supposedly might have defended the U.S. Mission at Benghazi) to stand down. According to the conspiracy theory, Hillary decided to sacrifice Ambassador Chris Stevens and four other Consulate officials for some unexplained ulterior motive or because of incompetence.

As with most accusations by Issa, the facts contradict him. As reported by the Huffington Post on July 11, 2014, nine military officers testified that a Special Operations Team in Tripoli could not have arrived in Benghazi in time to protect the Diplomatic Mission.

Other officers testified that confusing reports from Benghazi delayed relief for officials in the Benghazi annex, who were under fire after the attack on the main mission petered out. The situation in Tripoli on September 11-12, 2012, however, was also grave because of the Moslem unrest following the insulting American made video that caused riots in Cairo.

The Tripoli Embassy evacuated. Security personnel destroyed sensitive information and computer hard drives. The Special Operations Team in Tripoli consisted of four: a team leader, a medic, a communications specialist and an injured gunner, who had a foot in a cast. Chairman Issa has uncovered no facts that would tend to show that Secretary of State Clinton issued a stand down order. Trey Goudy can put on his evidence in the Select Committee show trial.

###

Democracy is worth dying for, because it is the most deeply honorable government ever devised by man.
Ronald Reagan

Chapter 3
One Citizen, One Vote?

Ronald Reagan was not typical of today's nihilists. Reagan believed in the sanctity of free elections. Nihilists are not willing to take election chances with America's changing demographics. Reagan grew up in an America dominated by folks who looked like Reagan. Ed Brooke (R-MA), an exception to the then prevailing rule, represented Massachusetts in the U. S. Senate from 1967 to 1979. Reagan never would have dreamed in 1970 that the GOP would nominate Brooke for president.

Thirty years after Brooke left the Senate, the junior Senator from Illinois, Barack Obama, took the oath of office as the first African American President of the U.S. in 2009. Demographics in the U.S., in the day of Reagan and Brooke, changed. The U.S. Census Bureau dropped a bombshell a few years ago. From 2011 on, the Census Bureau predicted that the majority of babies born in the U. S. would be to minority families.

Barack Obama's election in 2008 and the Census Bureau announcement in 2011 have had a profound effect on American politics. Two hundred and thirty years after their colonial antecedents harried the British, Tea Parties sprang up across America in response to the election of the first African American president.

Thirty states passed legislation to tighten up voting requirements and impose stricter voter ID procedures. Terms such as *Vote Suppression*, *Voter Intimidation* and *Voter Caging* are now in the general political lexicon. Why should nihilists waste hundreds of millions of dollars on advertising and campaigning for office, when Vote Suppression can deliver victory before the vote count can start.

It sounds innocent to ask people to identify themselves before they vote. There are millions of citizens, however, including African Americans, native Alaskans, the elderly and the poor, who have voted before without voter identification.

If an eighty year old shows up at the polls, she may not have a driver's license, a passport or a birth certificate in her purse. Precinct workers have seen the faces of many of these voters for years, and often know who they are. Stricter voter-ID requirements will not burden Mitt Romney, Governor Rick Scott (R-FL) or most of the residents of Palm Beach.

It is curious that the impetus for stricter voter ID laws coincided with the election of President Obama, spurred on by the Census Bureau announcement that, from and after 2011, the majority of babies born in the U. S. would be born to minority families. Nihilists no longer favor a path to citizenship for undocumented workers.

The Fourteenth Amendment to the U. S. Constitution does not allow for two classes of citizenship. That is exactly what nihilists want, however: (1) a Caucasian Class that runs business and government, and (2) an Undocumented Worker Class that picks America's fruits and vegetables, collects the trash, staffs the slaughterhouses, washes the dishes in the Nation's restaurants, and makes the beds and operates the laundries in the country's hotels and motels.

States with large black populations or large Hispanic populations adopted the strictest voting control laws. Historically, the Voting Rights Act of 1965 placed restrictions on nine mostly Southern States and some counties, north and south, and required application to the U. S. Justice Department before making any change in voting eligibility, precinct location or voting times.

Chief Justice John Roberts opined that the data showing discrimination was outdated. *Shelby County, Alabama v. Eric Holder* (2013) 570 U. S. ____. Texas and Mississippi, within hours of the decision, promised to enforce stricter voter ID laws that the Department of Justice has not approved. A batch of other states, north and south, prepared legislation to tighten voter ID laws.

If the U.S. deported all undocumented workers, America would shut down. Nihilists may argue that deportation of illegals will end our high unemployment problem. That is a pipedream. Guest workers perform the jobs that the rest of us cannot or will not do. Agricultural managers hire documented Americans to work the fields, only to see them walk away after toiling an hour or two in the sun. Some nihilists agree to allow guest workers to remain in the U.S., but want to deny them drivers' licenses, health care, and education benefits.

Nihilists want to create and benefit from a permanent slave class of second rate residents. Undocumented workers, however, surely will drive motor vehicles in America. Would it not be better to have every driver in a state take the state driver's test, and be licensed? Are we not concerned that the Nation's cooks might have tuberculosis or other communicable disease? Ignoring one group's medical care puts the health of the general population at risk. Why, if not to exploit their vulnerability, would it be better to keep one group more ignorant than the general population?

For a Nation of Immigrants, we seem to forget our pedigree. Governor Jan Brewer (R-AZ) seems oblivious to the fact that, when her ancestors got off the boat, Hispanic Americans in Arizona had direct relatives living there two hundred years earlier. Native Americans arrived eight thousand years before Jan Brewer's great grandmother.

When the Pilgrims landed at Plymouth Rock in 1620, without visas from the Americas, they met mostly friendly Native Americans. Natives showed the undocumented aliens how to fertilize seed corn with a fish to supply nitrogen. Natives showed the undocumented how to capture wild turkeys and use cranberries as a fruit.

A few years after Plymouth Landing, one of the leaders of the undocumented newcomers had a sit down with one of the Native Chiefs. The conversation was awkward for both sides. The leader of the undocumented explained that the undocumented recently established a Registry of Deeds. There are no words in the Native American language for *Registry of Deeds*.

The Native Chief could not comprehend what the leader of the undocumented was trying to say. The leader of the undocumented put it in simple terms. The undocumented *now own all the land that they want to claim, including land formerly occupied and used by Native Americans*. Native Americans may have use of some land that the undocumented do not claim. The Native American thought it strange that the newly arrived somehow owned all of the prime land, which Native Americans occupied for thousands of years.

In the State of Georgia, land speculators coveted land owned at least for hundreds of years by the Cherokee Nation. The legislature of Georgia surrendered without much of a fight to the land speculators, and, in concert with the Bureau of Indian Affairs, ordered the Cherokee Nation to pack-up and walk or ride to the Oklahoma Territory. Native Americans filed suit.

The U. S. Supreme Court refused to enjoin the State of Georgia from displacing Native Americans from their homeland. *Cherokee Nation v. the State of Georgia* (1831) 30 U.S. 1. The Court ruled that the Cherokee were not a foreign nation, over which the Constitution gave the Court jurisdiction. Arizona Governor Jan Brewer today merely wants her people to dominate over those she considers foreign. Forty years of Treaties between states and the United States with the Native Americans seemed worthless to the Natives in 1831 and thereafter.

Nihilism is gender neutral. Senator Kelly Ayotte (R-NH) is just as capable of hypocrisy as her male colleagues are, when she intones the mantra of *Four Dead Americans* to justify the Benghazi witch hunt. Marsha Blackburn (R-TN) usually finds a way to argue that President Obama is wrong on whatever policy is in question. Michele Bachmann (R-MN) is another kneejerk nihilist who opposes all things Obama. Bachmann sees herself as God's agent on earth, and follows God's suggestions in conducting her daily life, such as attending law school and running for president.

Bachmann's announcement of her intention not to seek re-election to the House in 2014, however, was inspired more by House Ethics Committee investigations, into her use of campaign funds in her 2012-run for president, than by Divine Providence. In June 2014, Tea Party candidate David Brat ousted Majority Leader Eric Cantor in a primary election. Brat seemed to say after his triumph that it was all part of God's plan. Brat may be Bachmann's replacement in the House. Cantor found solace in a three million dollar job on Wall Street as an investment banker.

Bachmann fought big government in a small way in Congress by sponsoring the *Light Bulb Freedom of Choice Act in 2010*. Bachmann decries big government largesse, but is first in line at the trough to benefit from government money for the Wisconsin farm that a Bachmann family partnership owns.

To take the heat off her family, Bachmann presently benefits only indirectly, while a tenant neighbor works the Bachmann farm and applies for farm subsidies. Marcus Bachmann's Christian Counseling Business (Bachmann & Associates) benefits from state and federal payments. The Bachmanns confirm that they do not pray away the gay.

The political platform approved by Governor Rick Perry (R-TX) and his nihilist followers included a provision to encourage so-called *reparative* therapy for gays. Perry explained as only he could explain. *I might have a gene that predisposes me to be an alcoholic, but I have free will not to drink.* According to Perry, you *can* pray away the gay. Perry later apologized for comparing gays to alcoholics.

Sarah Palin (R), unelected since walking away from her job as Governor of Alaska on July 26, 2009, is a nihilist cheerleader, a job which for which she has experience and aptitude. Bill Kristol, Editor of the *Weekly Standard*, endorsed Palin for Vice President early on in 2008. As usual with his maneuvers, it is difficult to know if Kristol embraced an atypical candidate to give the conservative ticket a boost or to increase circulation of his *Weekly Standard* periodical.

Unable to find an acceptable running mate in 2008 from Maine to California or from Minnesota to Texas, Senator John McCain (R-AZ) went all the way to Wasilla, Alaska, to find an acceptable candidate for Vice President. Palin brought excitement and novelty to the ticket, accusing Barack Obama of associating with terrorists. Candidate Obama at the time sat on some boards with Bill Ayers, who was a bomb thrower against the Viet Nam War in the 1960s. Palin may have coined the term *Death Panel* to scare Americans away from the *Affordable Care Act.*

In 2009, Palin released her memoir *Going Rogue* to highlight her personal struggle to escape the iron control of her 2008 campaign handlers, Steve Schmidt and Nicolle Wallace, both of whom admitted after the election defeat that Palin was not ready for *Prime Time.* When she asked permission to give a concession speech, the Campaign staff instructed Palin that

Vice Presidential candidates do not give concession speeches.

The genie went back into the bottle, but she would not stay there for long. The tension between Palin and the McCain campaign, as depicted in the book and movie, *Game Change*, resulted from an unscripted player reacting predictably in an unpredictable manner to a tightly scripted campaign strategy. Palin was supposed to bring a breath of fresh air to McCain's lack luster campaign. Once nominated, her handlers throttled Palin.

Ronald Reagan believed that democracy was worth dying for. Folks who are the victims of Vote Suppression or who have to wait in line six hours to vote do not believe that rigged elections are worth dying for. Political parties often lapse into excesses on both sides. There are few examples, however, of progressives patrolling upscale neighborhoods to intimidate and suppress the vote of the wealthy.

Reince Priebus, Chair, Republican National Committee, and his political operatives, use voters' ZIP Codes to gauge if a voter is likely to be a progressive, whose vote is dangerous to the right. Nihilists have adopted voter intimidation and vote suppression as tools of the political trade. The excuse given is that the individuals targeted for challenge somehow look foreign, and, possibly are not citizens eligible to vote. White, Anglo-Saxon men seem to be most at ease in the environment of the Republican Party. The GOP does not appreciate the *"huddled masses, yearning to breathe free"*.

Nihilists approach politics the same as marketing any other product. Nihilist candidates for office beyond one State or Congressional District are becoming chameleons, who can and do change their political color to match the background of the neighborhood of the day. Mitt Romney was an expert at waffling and flip-flopping. In progressive districts, Romney was a middle of the road pragmatist. In nihilist districts, Romney praised Ronald Reagan.

How could Romney sponsor health care with an individual mandate in Massachusetts in 2006, recommend his plan as the model for a national compulsory health care scheme, and campaign against Barack Obama in 2012 as a fierce opponent of the *Affordable Care Act*? Rick Santorum was not the only one who saw Romney's position as conflicted, inconsistent and untenable.

What is truly remarkable is that Romney is staking himself out as a dark horse in 2016. There is only one reason Romney continues his attacks on President Obama and *Affordable Care*. Romney is desperate to maintain relevance with the nihilists, who just might choose the master chameleon at a deadlocked convention to run against Hillary.

Romney has his explanation ready for his contorted health care position. One size does not fit all. Washington cannot mandate health care to fifty sovereign states. The states are laboratories for democracy—except where vote suppression and gerrymandered districts tilt the outcome in favor of nihilists.

Justice Antonin Scalia questions voting as a racial entitlement

"Whenever a society adopts racial entitlements, it is very difficult to get them out through the normal political process."

U. S. Supreme Court Justice Antonin Scalia at Oral Argument in *Shelby County v. Holder.*

Beware! Even the great originalist, U. S. Supreme Court Justice, Antonin Scalia, appears perplexed by lack of Congressional opposition to reauthorization of the *Voting Rights Act of 1965*, which Justice Scalia imagines might be a Racial Entitlement. Despite the Justice's concerns, Voting is not a Racial Entitlement. Voting is a fundamental right held by every U. S. citizen irrespective of race, color or creed.

The United States abolished slavery by the Thirteenth Amendment. Written with the ink of patriots and in the blood of 600,000 fallen, the Nation belatedly covenanted that, *"All persons born or naturalized in the United States, and subject to the jurisdiction thereof, are citizens of the United States and of the state wherein they reside."* The Fourteenth Amendment defined and conferred citizenship—without regard to race or previous condition of servitude.

Justice Scalia has it backwards, and wants to invalidate laws that protect voting because the discrimination prohibited in the 21st Century may not be as blatant or as pervasive as it was under the Confederate Battle Flag in the 19th Century or in the 20th Century.

Nor is it is a racial entitlement for a dwindling white majority to seek to disenfranchise or disadvantage Blacks or other minorities. And the right to vote cannot be dismissed as some sort of special and unwarranted privilege persisting by virtue of race, and perpetuated by a rubber-stamp Congress that, in the opinion of Justice Scalia, has forfeited its status as a co-equal branch of government.

The Attorney General of the genteel State of Alabama gratuitously offered to weed out superfluous federal civil rights laws. Congress passed, and President Lyndon Johnson signed into law, the *Voting Rights Act of 1965 "to enforce the fifteenth amendment to the Constitution of the United States". "The right of citizens of the United States to vote shall not be denied or abridged by the United States or by any state on account of race, color, or previous condition of servitude."*

It is a measure of the Republican Party's abandonment of Civil Rights that Congress did not pass the Voting Rights Act eighty years earlier. Republicans, of course, rapidly tired of championing the recently emancipated after the Civil War, as demonstrated by the 1877 *Hayes-Tilden* pact that ended the electoral standoff of 1876.

Civil Rights enforcement and enjoyment may be compared to the precarious status of a ping pong ball held up, against the relentless downward pull of gravity, prejudice and custom, by water squirting upwards from a garden hose. When the water spigot is turned off, the ball drops precipitously. The federal government is the water. Congress is the hose. The Constitution, the Law and the good sense of the American People hold the hand on the water faucet.

When the Republicans tired of Civil Rights in 1877, the Nation dropped the Civil Rights ball for nearly ninety years. The Attorneys General of Alabama, Mississippi, South Carolina and Texas, no longer took up arms against Blacks. They used a more insidious weapon, commonly referred to as "the Law".

South Carolina and Texas had an interesting, but not, unusual, tactic for the South, in their voting procedures. Democrats controlled Southern States from the precinct house to the State Capitol. The winner of the Democratic Primary would be the ultimate winner of any election, come hell or high water.

The general election was meaningless. The good ole boys in Columbia and Austin amended the state constitution or enacted laws to keep southern gentility alive. *It seems that Blacks, for some esoteric reason, were deemed not qualified to vote in the Democratic Primary.* The Democratic Party in South Carolina or Texas, after all, was a Club. *Any self-respecting Club has a God-given right to determine its members' qualifications.* To show that there was no prejudice at work in banning Blacks, as a group, from the electoral process, South Carolina and Texas allowed Blacks to vote in the general election—*where their vote often was meaningless*. Other Southern States adopted the same approach. The political parties were private organizations, which could select their members.

Despite the post Civil War Amendments to the U. S. Constitution, Republicans threw blacks under the bus starting in 1877. Democrats split on civil rights after the Hayes-Tilden sell-out. Southern Democrats gave thanks as they restored the gentility of the lily white, ante-bellum, South. Democrats below the Mason-Dixon Line disenfranchised blacks by enacting poll taxes or by using ignorant Voter Registrars to inform unschooled Freedmen that, as Blacks, they required an advanced level of understanding of state constitutional law to vote.

Gradually, after nearly ninety years of neglect, the National Democratic Party came to realize that the Nation needed to enforce Civil Rights for all citizens. Congress passed the *Civil Rights Act of 1964* to prevent discrimination in public facilities, including transportation.

Southern Democrats (before the Great Migration of White Southerners to the GOP) filibustered the bill for months. Rosa Parks, whose statue was unveiled in the Halls of Congress years later in 2013, ultimately could ride in the front of the bus without a lot of fuss (and without being subject to arrest for riding while Black).

There was now a stream of water holding up the delicately balanced ping pong ball. Lyndon Johnson picked up the baton from an assassinated President Kennedy in 1963. Johnson predicted that the Democrats would lose the South with the passage of the *Voting Rights Act of 1965*. The migration of Whites to the Republican Party became a stampede. It took a Civil War, the loss of six hundred thousand lives, the 13th, 14th and 15th Amendments to the U. S. Constitution and the *Voting Right Act of 1965* to start to put an end to *Jim Crow* laws designed by conservatives to disenfranchise Blacks.

Section 5 of the Act requires the genteel, formerly rebellious, Southern States and some counties, north and south, to obtain pre-clearance from the U. S. Justice Department before implementing a change in "any voting qualification or prerequisite to voting, or standard, practice, or procedure with respect to voting". Southern gentility generally abhors superfluous federal laws, especially laws that supervise voting rights of African Americans.

The Attorney General of the Genteel State of Alabama earnestly seeks to invalidate the *Voting Rights Act of 1965* and section 5 because they are no longer needed. Southern gentility and Black enfranchisement are no longer mutually exclusive terms. Representative Lynn Westmoreland (R-GA) spoke eloquently, *if dishonestly*, to the issue:

"Congress is declaring from on high that states with voting problems 40 years ago can simply never be forgiven, that Georgians must eternally wear the scarlet letter because of the actions of their grandparents and great grandparents. We have repented and we have reformed."

If anything, however, the problem with GOP attempts to disenfranchise voters is becoming worse in the 21st Century, not better. The subversion of voting rights is no longer just southern gentility against Blacks. The entire apparatus of the Republican Party is engaged in a nationwide struggle to disenfranchise progressive voters, principally Democrats.

The GOP is in a death spiral as the result of changing demographics. Instead of cleaning up their act to allow easier entrance to *Dumbo's* tent, the GOP is using ZIP codes to identify and exclude progressives and minorities from the voting booth, north and south.

Mike Turzai, Speaker of the Pennsylvania Assembly was ecstatic (caught on U-Tube) in 2012 as he [i]proclaimed, *"Voter ID, done, which is going to allow Governor Romney to win the State of Pennsylvania."*

Governor Rick Scott (R-FL) made Katherine Harris look like a piker, at least at his first attempt to remove suspected progressives and minorities from the voter rolls. As Secretary of State (and Co-Chair of Bush's Campaign), Harris purged about 5,000 progressives from Florida's voter rolls to enable her ultimately to declare George W. Bush the winner by *537 votes* in the 2000 election. Bush became President with Florida's disputed electoral votes, despite losing the popular vote to Al Gore by more than 550,000 votes.

Chief Justice William H. Rehnquist and the Right Wing majority on the Supreme Court stopped a recount ordered by the Florida Supreme Court, and "voted" Bush president by a single vote of five over four Justices. Governor Scott wanted to purge 180,000 progressive voters to tilt the 2012 election in Mitt Romney's favor. Under the glare of public scrutiny, Scott settled for a purge of only 2,700 names from the voter rolls. Governor Scott claims he just wanted "fair elections".

In the midst of this toxic assault on Democracy, the Attorney General of the Genteel State of Alabama, in *Shelby County v. Holder*, sued to invalidate Section 5 *as no longer needed*. To cap off a bizarre situation, Associate U. S. Supreme Court Justice Antonin Scalia, at Oral Argument, apparently thought Alabama might be right.

Scalia fears that the Congress votes periodically to re-authorize the *Voting Rights Act of 1965* out of some sort of legislative inertia, which Scalia seems ready to cure with a dose of Right Wing judicial activism. It seems dangerous to Scalia that *no Senator and only few Representatives* voted against the last enactment of the *Civil Rights Act of 1965*. At Oral Argument, Scalia apparently thought he and the Right Wing Justices should act because Congress was in a *Politically Correct* rut.

"Now, I don't think that's attributable to the fact that it is so much clearer now that we need this. I think it is attributable, very likely attributable, to a phenomenon that is called perpetuation of racial entitlement. It's been written about. Whenever a society adopts racial entitlements, it is very difficult to get out of them through the normal political process." Justice Antonin Scalia at oral argument in *Shelby County v. Holder*.

Justice Scalia, of course, is brilliantly provocative as always. For example, it took World War II to end the racial entitlement of the Aryan Purists in the *Fatherland*. Judicial Activism, of the type contemplated by Justice Scalia, failed to root out Racial Entitlements in Germany or Italy in the 1930s.

The *Reichstag* abdicated and allowed the Leader of the Executive Branch to make his own laws by passing the *Enabling Act of 1933*. Taking a cue from the rationale embraced by Justice Scalia, about the danger of legislators mechanically voting politically correct, Benito Mussolini simply abolished the Italian Parliament in 1939.

Justice Scalia wants to bypass the U. S. Congress, at least, where he sees the peril of unchecked racial entitlement and the inertia of Political Correctness apparently causing paralysis in the Legislative Branch. Just maybe, however, American Democracy needs a different path.

Talking heads are already looking to Justice Kennedy as the potential *Swing Vote* to prevent Clarence Thomas from teaming up with Scalia, Alioto and the Chief Justice to strike down the *Voting Rights Act of 1965* as unconstitutional because vote suppression and voter intimidation miraculously have gone away.

These same pundits saw the *Affordable Care Act* ("ACA") doomed unless Justice Kennedy swung his vote to the rescue in the 2012 Supreme Court decision in *National Federation of Independent Business v. Sebelius*. At the end of the day, however, it was Chief Justice John Roberts, and not Justice Kennedy, who voted with the progressives to save the ACA. If Justice Kennedy votes to gut the *Voting Rights Act of 1965*, the Chief Justice should vote with the progressives again.

No Chief Justice of John Roberts' stature could allow the Genteel State of Alabama to put in peril the enfranchisement of a large segment of the American population. In the words of John Lewis, whom Sheriff's Deputies and State Troopers allowed to be beaten nearly to death in the *Freedom March* with Martin Luther King at the *Edmund Pettus Bridge*, Selma, Alabama, on March 7, 1965, *"We are not going back"*. Governor Wallace ordered law enforcement to stop the Freedom Riders to preserve "public safety". (Wallace also favored preservation of the genteel life).

Justice Roberts supported Shelby County, Alabama's lawsuit. The statistics showing discrimination were outdated. States' Rights have been vindicated, and personal rights suppressed.

What we are witnessing now is living history. The events are not as exciting as the attack on Fort Sumter by the Genteel State of South Carolina on April 14, 1861, or Pickett's brutal sacrifice at Gettysburg on July 3, 1863, or the attack on Freedom Marchers at Selma, Alabama, on March 7, 1965. The insidious attack and subversion of democracy by the GOP in the 21st Century, however, is more sinister and potentially more dangerous than was the Rebellion in 1860 or the blatant racism of the 19th and 20th Centuries.

That U. S. Supreme Court Justice Anton Scalia would refer to the Right to Vote as a *racial entitlement* (to get out of), is a *chilling* reminder that the Nation has a long way to go before Equal Law and Justice under the Constitution is achieved. The unelected United States Supreme Court Justices should reject Scalia's thesis that the elected Congress is incapable of sorting out what laws are needed to enfranchise the American People at the voting booth.

Scalia maintained at Oral Argument that the issue could not be addressed through *"normal political process"*. What Scalia suggests is an *abnormal and unlawful subversion* of the Constitution and the gutting of a Law, enacted by the People's Representatives, by a sometime Right Wing Majority of the U. S. Supreme Court. Scalia has impeached himself. Scalia no longer deserves to be taken seriously.

Georgia Representative Lynn Westmoreland suggests, *supra*, that there is no discrimination in the South. When asked to compare Michelle Obama with John McCain's selection of Sara Palin for Vice President, Westmoreland said, *"Just from what little I've seen of her and Mr. Obama, they're a member of an elitist class of individuals that thinks that they're uppity"*.

It is painfully obvious that Westmoreland thinks the Obamas are uppity. (A *Black* Family in the *White* House? *What will they think of next?*) Westmoreland was one of two Representatives to vote against the *Emmett Till Bill* to fund FBI investigations of killings during the Civil Rights era.

Westmoreland is vehemently opposed to Democrats gerrymandering Congressional Districts. He led the fight as Republican Leader in the Georgia House to stop Democrats from mapping a skewed redistricting in 2001. After the Republicans took control of the Georgia House in 2004, Westmoreland thought GOP gerrymandering was fine. If the Attorney General of Alabama can come up with witnesses to equality only such as Lynn Westmoreland, the suit by Shelby County is in trouble. Westmoreland is not a witness in Court, but just asking.

Westmoreland could be a poster boy for the genteel politician in the South. Westmoreland has a high school education and believes in a libertarian life. Westmoreland is not impressed with uppity people—the Obamas, for example. Westmoreland could be a chicken hawk, if he wanted to, because he never served in the U. S. military. To show his Christian Coalition credentials, Westmoreland co-sponsored a bill to place the Ten Commandments in the U. S. House and Senate.

Westmoreland also submitted a bill to allow state courthouses to display the Ten Commandments in a historical setting. On the *Stephen Colbert Show*, Westmoreland appeared to have a difficult time naming more than three of the Ten Commandments. Westmoreland opposed renewing Section 5 of the *Voting Rights Act of 1965* that required many Southern States and some counties, north and south, to obtain pre-clearance from the U. S. Justice Department to change voting qualifications.

###

An imbalance between rich and poor is the oldest and most fatal ailment of all republics.
Plato

Chapter 4
Fear of Redistribution

After the Select Committee on Benghazi shamelessly tries to frighten Hillary Clinton away from politics with the specter of *Four Dead Americans*, the theory is that nihilist candidates will be able to puff themselves up and be able to beat the nominee of the progressives in November 2016. A look at the nihilist kennel, however, suggests that none of these dogs will hunt. Each nihilist want-to-be president is conflicted and fatally flawed. The flaws start out more as policy flaws, but ultimately call character into question as Republicans mislead the People.

Nihilists have to pretend that they do not really support the policies they support. Or they flip flop on policies, depending on which way the wind is blowing at the time. Mitt Romney's countless flips on national health care should win him an Olympic Gold Medal. Romney picked up the baton on health care from Richard Nixon and the heritage Foundation, and signed Romney Care into law as Massachusetts Governor in 2006.

Romney Care included an individual mandate that required broad public participation in health insurance coverage. Romney recommended that Romney Care be the model for a national health care plan with an individual mandate. Nihilists more or less accepted the legitimacy of Romney Care.

Barack Obama followed Romney's advice, and used Romney Care as a model for a national healthcare law with an individual mandate. As soon as President Obama adopted a healthcare plan that the Republicans supported since 1973, nihilists became hysterical in their opposition. Romney dearly wanted the presidency in 2012. Sensing that the nihilists would not soon abandon their compulsive opposition, Romney condemned the *Affordable Care Act*. Rick Santorum had one thing right in the 2012 campaign.

Romney was the "worst person" to lead the charge against *Affordable Care* for the American People. Romney's flips on healthcare were so nuanced that it seemed at times that the impetus for enacting Romney Care came more the Massachusetts Legislature than from the Governor. Romney went so far as to claim he did not recommend his healthcare plan as the model for a national healthcare plan. By the time the American People saw the video of Romney alleging that 47% of the electorate were freeloaders, a majority of the voters did not believe Romney in 2012.

Santorum hopes to pick up in 2016 where he left off in 2012. Santorum gave Romney a run for his money in 2012, but Romney's money and organization overwhelmed Santorum. The primary among nihilists was as much a religious crusade as a political campaign. Many Protestants viewed Romney's Mormon faith with distrust. Despite being Catholic, Santorum's family values campaign resonated with fundamental Christians. Santorum lost progressives with his anti-abortion and anti-gay agenda.

When asked about changing the military's *Don't Ask, Don't Tell* policy on gays, Santorum ducked the question by saying that sex has no place in the military. Senator Marco Rubio (R-FL) will be an interesting study in 2016. Rubio sponsored an Immigration Bill in 2013. Rubio favored a pathway to citizenship for "undocumented workers". Rubio, of course, had his eye on Hispanic voters, many of whom have relatives or friends who are waiting for a pathway to citizenship. The Tea Party, however, opposed a pathway to citizenship for illegals. Undocumented workers might work in the U.S., but could not become citizens.

Sensing that the base would support the Tea Party position, Rubio flipped and opposed his own Immigration Bill. Rubio dreamed of a Hispanic Tsunami sweeping him into power from coast to coast. The tidal wave of support for Rubio would begin in Miami, he thought, with the Cubans who have voted for nihilists since President John F. Kennedy abandoned the Bay of

Pigs invasion in 1961. The illusory Dade County swell for Rubio was supposed to coalesce with Spanish speakers across the land.

Turns out that Miami Cubans no longer vote the same as their grandfathers. Rubio will likely carry most Miami Cubans over the age of 78. Rubio's flip flops on immigration will leave him without Hispanic support nationwide.

Mitt Romney still desperately wants to be president. Why else does Romney continue to speak out against the *Affordable Care Act*, a national health care plan that replicates Romney Care? Romney continues to try to ingratiate himself with the nihilist base. Romney does not dare to actively campaign for president a third time. However, if a sincere draft Romney movement develops at a deadlocked convention, Romney will volunteer to run a third time. Gingrich may also run in 2016.

His own party fired Gingrich as Speaker of the House in 1999. Gingrich uses politics the same way as does former New York Mayor Rudolf Giuliani, to gain publicity to make money by consulting. Gingrich needs funds to justify his $500,000 revolving charge at Tiffany's.

While preaching faithfulness to Bill Clinton in 1998 (and urging impeachment over a fib under oath about an affair), Gingrich was having his own dalliances while his wife lay dying. Henry Hyde (R-IL), a House Impeachment Manager in 1998, since deceased, thought it was grossly unfair of the press to bring up Hyde's twenty-year-old infidelity.

The moral is that the accused should know who the target of a witch hunt is, and stop bringing up irrelevant issues like the morals of the accusers. Nihilists constituted the Select Committee on Benghazi to smear Hillary Clinton. Progressives should not disrupt the proceeding with facts that might bring out the truth. Another nihilist dark horse for 2016 is John McCain, who also desperately wants to be president. Why else would McCain automatically oppose all things Obama? McCain is doing the same thing Romney is doing. Both are appeasing the nihilist base.

Follow the Money

It is inevitable that the governed will vote their pocketbooks in an attempt to protect their perceived economic interests. There are other factors in play, however, to explain the agitated reaction some Tea Partiers exhibit towards President Obama, who has been called a Dictator, a Kenyan, a King, a Moslem, a Marxist, a Socialist and a Traitor. As entrepreneurs, the opposition of Tea Partiers reaches fever pitch. If business is bad, it's Obama's fault. If business is good, it would be better without Obama. Republicans present the *Affordable Care Act* as a job killer.

Underlying all of the Tea Partiers' hype against the President is an unrealistic fear of redistribution of wealth. According to Tea Partiers, President Obama views himself as a modern day Robin Hood who would take from the haves to make life better for the have-nots. Most of the Tea Partiers, however, do not have that much wealth. Maybe that is why they are on the verge of hysteria. It would be understandable for nihilist opposition to come from millionaires and billionaires such as Charles and David Koch, Sheldon Adelson, and Mitt Romney.

Internal Revenue Taxes inevitably result in redistribution of wealth. America's founders were not advocates of redistribution of wealth by government. Charity in the eighteenth century was for the beneficence of individuals or religions. That is why the U. S. Constitution provided for an internal revenue tax based only on a per capita assessment or required tax to apportion among the states according to population.

The adoption of the Sixteenth Amendment in 1913 allowed direct taxation of income without apportionment. Graduated tax rates early on gave redistributive effect to income taxation. The United States experienced social approval of a meritocracy, where individuals could rise above their economic class through education or hard work, or both. In the 1960s, some colleges charged tuition of $500 a semester.

In 2014, the cost of tuition for a semester was more like $15,000. Working part time while at school or full time in the summer cannot defray the cost of higher education today. Aristocracy is rapidly replacing the meritocracy. The upper one percent can afford the cost of college, no matter how high those costs would go.

Perils of Loss of Class Mobility

America still celebrates its Horatio Alger dreams, where the impoverished can rise through hard work and perseverance. Class stasis is becoming the reality in the U.S., as if rigor mortis has overtaken social mobility. The American Revolution preceded the French Revolution by nearly eighteen years. In eighteenth century France, class stasis was cast, if not in concrete, in equally unyielding mud. The upper one percent lived a life that was a fairy tale until the Reign of Terror meted out death indiscriminately, not for capital offenses, but merely for membership in the most privileged social class.

Without sounding too maudlin, would the French Revolution have been averted by a graduated income tax, social security, Medicare, Medicaid and affordable education for the masses? Anyone born in the mud in France in 1750 knew they would live in the mud, work in the mud, marry in the mud, raise children in the mud and be buried in a mud covered grave beside a muddy path to nowhere. The hopelessness of the life of a French peasant burst into vibrant dreams with a tint of red, as the yoke of the one percent was violently overthrown.

Life today in twenty-first century France and Europe celebrates the meritocracy rather than the aristocracy. Admittance to university is not a privilege of the wealthy. Tea Partiers in the U.S., however, rail that Obama is moving the U.S. towards European Socialism.

The Tea Party wants to shrink government. Do they really want the social class stasis that might follow the policies of an indifferent, laissez-faire government? Nihilists howl that the market should determine what businesses survive. Tea Partiers opposed the bank bailout sponsored by

George W. Bush in 2008. Let bad banks fail they said. But when Lehman Brothers failed on September 15, 2008, with six hundred billion dollars in assets, the American banking system collapsed.

Barclays Bank offered to buy Lehman's core business, but the Bank of England and British regulators required consent of shareholders of Lehman, UK, before any sale of Lehman's assets. Bank of America offered to step in, to no avail, if the U. S. government would absorb some of the losses. The market, indeed, worked its will. Credit in the U.S. and throughout the world dried up. Mortgage lending all but vanished. The Housing market fell like a house of cards. Upwards of fifteen million Americans lost their jobs. Tea Partiers should have been ecstatic at the brute efficiency of the market. George W. Bush and even many nihilists, however, decided that a bank bailout was preferable to a second Great Depression.

###

If they have no bread, let them eat cake.

attributed to Marie Antoinette

Chapter 5
Contract On America

Nihilists prevailed at the polls in 1994, and took over the U.S. House of Representatives for the first time in 40 years. They vowed they would never be left out in the wilderness again. Newt Gingrich (R-GA) rallied nihilist troops, and was elected Speaker of the House. The revolution was well planned. Before the '94 election, Gingrich and Richard Armey (R-TX) released a document entitled, *Contract With America*, based in part on Ronald Reagan's 1985 State of the Union Address to Congress. The *Contract* was the nihilists' promise of what they would do for America if they took control.

After seeing what the nihilists did and threatened to do in policy matters, critics have renamed it, *Contract On America*. For details of present nihilists' policy, *see* Fiscal Year 2015 Budget Resolution, *The Path to Prosperity*, prepared by Paul Ryan (R-WI) and adopted by the nihilists in the House. Here is the nihilist agenda to do away with social programs and increase military spending, only some of which are described in the Ryan Budget, a/k/a *Path to* [Koch Brothers'] *Prosperity*.

• Social Security: privatize (and risk pension loss in the stock market)

• Medicare & Medicaid: reduce benefits and replace with vouchers

• Minimum Wage: Repeal

• Affordable Healthcare: Repeal [and replace with rhetoric and sleight of hand]

• Veterans' Services: privatize

• Taxes: minimize to starve the beast of government and cut back social programs

• Immigration: seal the border; oppose path to citizenship for undocumented workers

• Food Stamps: reduce, or eliminate, or shift to states with block grants

• Defense Spending: increase

- Elections: challenge moderate conservatives in primaries, and outspend progressives
- Aid For Dependent Children: shift to states with block grants
- Education funding: eliminate or severely limit federal subsidies
- Jobs Bills: block and string out the recession to make Obama look bad
- Infrastructure Bills: block and allow the U.S to become a third world country
- All things Obama: hysterically oppose to minimize or destroy any chance of a legacy
- Democracy: defuse by vote suppression, stricter voter ID and voter intimidation
- Benghazi: mock the *Four Dead Americans* with a political smear of Hillary Clinton
- Congress: waste a chance to help America with 50 bills to cripple *Affordable Healthcare*
- Military: privatize noncombat functions such as logistics, food service, medical, & fuel
- Taxation: no corporate tax; lower tax on rich; increase taxes on poor and middle class
- U.S. Postal Service: destroy with burden of 75 years of pension funds charged in five years
- Workers' Unions: marginalize; prohibit strikes by public employees

Voters should reject the nihilist agenda. Voters should reject nihilists because their policies favor the top one percent at the expense of everyone else. Two factors distort today's voting fairness. The decennial election of 2010 had a profound effect on nihilist control of state legislatures and state and federal voting districts.

Since nihilists controlled many more states than did progressives, nihilists were able to gerrymander election districts to make a majority safe for nihilist candidates from 2011-2020. Nihilist-controlled states are able to enact stricter voter ID laws and allow vote suppression and voter intimidation to hold down progressive votes. Democracy and the normal rule of the majority are sacrificed to the oligarchy of the nihilists, the Ryan Budget and the *Path to* [Koch Brothers'] *Prosperity*.

Congressman Ryan's *Path to Prosperity* (*"Path"*) is full of distortions. Ryan claims the Congressional Budget Office ("CBO") found that the *Affordable Care Act* "will discourage work". *Plan*, p. 9. The CBO estimated that *some* workers will choose to work fewer hours if their health insurance is not tied to their job. CBO, Budget and Economic Outlook, Appendix "C", p. 117. Nihilists extrapolated the CBO comment to mean that the *Affordable Care Act* is a "Job Killer". Curiously, Romney Care is not a job killer in Massachusetts.

Romney defended the individual mandate because there is no "free ride". Everyone, according to Romney, has to pay for the cost run up by uninsured, who ultimately take treatment in hospital emergency rooms.

It was only after President Obama embraced the forty year dream of Richard Nixon and the Heritage Foundation for mandatory healthcare that nihilists became hysterical in their opposition. Opponents of *Affordable Care* were certain that the Act would be struck down as unconstitutional. The rationale was that the government cannot force the American People to buy a product or a service.

This rationale ignored federal laws that require purchase of helmets for motorcycle use, seatbelts for automobiles and state laws that require public liability insurance in states that have compulsory automobile insurance. Chief Justice John Roberts surprised everyone by upholding the Act.

Affordable Care passed constitutional muster under the federal government's taxing power, not under the Commerce Clause. *National Federation of Independent Business [and Twenty-Six States] v. Sebelius, Secretary of Human Health and Services*, June 28, 2012. 567 U.S. ____ .

Chief Justice John Roberts reasoned that the Commerce Clause authorized Congress to regulate interstate commerce activities. People who do not purchase health insurance are not engaged in interstate activity simply by not purchasing healthcare insurance. In Roberts' opinion, the Commerce Clause cannot sustain the *Affordable Care Act*. However, Roberts (and four progressive Justices) ruled that the government can tax people who refuse to purchase health insurance. The progressive Justices, in an opinion written by Justice Ginsberg, argued that the Commerce Clause also authorized the *Affordable Care Act*.

Nihilists were dumbfounded. The Chief Justice, nominated by George W. Bush, single-handedly saved Obama's signature healthcare initiative. Had Chief Justice Roberts voted against *Affordable Care*, the Act would have been ruled unconstitutional.

###

It's Déjà Vu All Over Again

Rep. Ron Paul, 10/8/03, opposing HR 1828-03, a bill to control Syria and Lebanon

.

Chapter 6
Groundhog Day

Every morning since January 20, 2009, Senator John McCain wakes up at 6:00 AM and looks for a camera to renew his criticism of President Obama's foreign policy. If posing for pictures helped Ronald Reagan to the White House, why would it not work for McCain? It does not matter what McCain says from day to day or year to year, as long as he can find a camera today and accuse the President of feckless foreign policy. McCain at one point opined that the U. S. should close Guantánamo Prison because it gives terrorists a rallying cry. A soon as President Obama took steps to close Guantánamo, McCain proclaimed that U.S. security would be in peril without this one detention center located at the southeastern tip of Cuba.

For McCain every day will be *Groundhog Day*, until January 20, 2017, when President Obama leaves office. As a nihilist leader, John McCain is locked in the time warp of compulsive criticism of Obama's foreign policy. The chaos in Iraq in June 2014, however, led to a return of the ghosts who planned and executed the 2003

Invasion of Iraq. ISIS (Islamic Forces in Iraq and Syria), forced out of Syria, turned on Iraq, captured Mosul and threatened Baghdad. The U. S. architects of the destabilization of Iraq in 2003 all came forward to defend their errors and recommend a redo of the very policies that tore Iraq apart.

Only one of the sponsors of the 2003 Invasion of Iraq maintained a dignified silence. President George W. Bush decided early on when he left office in January 2009 that he would not take pot shots at his successor. Vice President Cheney feels that he must tear President Obama down to prove that Cheney's folly in 2003 was justified.

Cheney claims that President Obama planned to take the U. S. down a notch with feeble policy. All of the other Iraq War Plan malefactors have joined Cheney in a Greek Chorus, warning of the peril of not endorsing their misadventure. In a political version of the Rocky Horror Picture Show, all the miscreants have come out. Dick Cheney, Paul Wolfowitz, L Paul Bremer and Bill Kristol are on Talk Shows telling the American People how President Obama lost Iraq.

Wolfowitz, of course, prepared the Plan to Invade Iraq in *1992* (entitled *Defense Panning Guidance*) when he was Under Secretary of Defense for Policy reporting to Secretary of Defense Dick Cheney. In 1992, Wolfowitz raised the specter of Weapons of Mass Destruction in Iraq. Before the election in 2000, George W. Bush made a spectacular mistake that would destine his presidency to fail. Bush appointed Cheney head of the selection team to choose a

Vice President. After careful consideration, Cheney chose himself as Vice President.

Bush followed up with another colossal mistake. Bush made Cheney head of the transition team that would select trusted officials in the Government, particularly the Departments of Defense and State. The People elected Bush President, but Cheney would run the country—at least until the debacle of 2003 Iraq War caused Bush to put a leash on his Vice President during the second term.

Cheney lined up the Neoconservatives ("Neocons") to take over the U.S. Government. Cheney installed Donald Rumsfeld as Secretary of Defense. Wolfowitz came back as Deputy Secretary of Defense, bringing the Iraq War Plan with him. Irwin ("Scooter") Libby assisted Wolfowitz in writing the Iraq War Plan at DoD in 1992. Libby became Cheney's Chief of Staff.

Douglas Feith, who worked for DoD in the Reagan years, came in under Wolfowitz as Head of *Special Plans* at DoD. The *Special Plan* was the 2003 Invasion of Iraq. When the Central Intelligence Agency dragged its feet on "finding" facts that would support the existence of Weapons of Mass Destruction in Iraq, Cheney and Libby made repeated trips to Langley, Virginia, to educate CIA analysts about what facts CIA should "find".

War with Iraq needed a justification. Saddam Hussein's alleged possession of Weapons of Mass Destruction would be the casus belli. Cheney, Rumsfeld and Wolfowitz needed someone respectable to "prove" to a sober world audience that Iraq possessed Weapons of Mass Destruction (WMD). Cheney and Scooter Libby had already instructed CIA analysts as to what damning "facts" CIA should find to support a conclusion of WMD. Secretary of State Colin Powell was the most respected member of the team because he was the opposite of the other players. Powell was not a chicken hawk like Wolfowitz.

Powell was not a neocon like Rumsfeld. Powell was not a manipulator like Cheney. Unlike George W. Bush, Powell was not a born again Christian who could embrace the Invasion of Iraq as a matter of faith. Powell addressed the United Nations on February 5, 2003, and presented "facts" that were invented or embellished by Dick Cheney. To give credence to the dog and pony show orchestrated by Cheney, but delivered by Powell, CIA Director George Tenet sat in the row of seats behind Powell. Powell presented to the U.N. what he believed was irrefutable proof of WMD in Iraq.

Powell presented a computer image of an Iraqi mobile unit, alleged to be a biological weapons lab. This claim depended in part on false information supplied by Rafid al-Janabi, a/k/a "Curveball", an Iraqi immigrant living in Germany. Powell presented evidence that Iraq had aluminum tubes for uranium processing. Experts had cautioned the CIA that the tubes were more likely for use in Iraq's artillery than for use in a nuclear weapons program. Cheney made sure that Powell was unaware of countervailing evidence. Powell's presentation to the U.N. supported a conclusion that Iraq possessed WMD.

At the urging of Cheney, Powell presented unreliable evidence that tried to link Iraq with al-Qaeda and the attack on the World Trade Center and the Pentagon on 9/11/01. Colonel Lawrence B. Wilkerson, Chief of Staff to Secretary of State Colin Powell, explains that he and Powell had scant time to evaluate the facts invented by Cheney, that the Iraq War intelligence was a hoax and that he and Colin Powell were unaware of the facts when Powell made the presentation to the U.N.

The course of history likely would have been radically different if George W. Bush had not allowed Cheney to take over the U. S. Government during Bush's first term in office. Planning the Invasion of Iraq did not occur in 2002. Cheney, Wolfowitz and Scooter Libby included the Invasion of Iraq in the Defense Policy Guidance of 1992.

Once Bush allowed Cheney free reign, the 2003 Invasion of Iraq was a foregone conclusion. In 2002, Rumsfeld took the 1992 Wolfowitz Plan off the shelf, dusted it off and prepared the 2003 Invasion of Iraq. Everything the Neocons said or promised about the Iraq fiasco was wrong. Rumsfeld thought a U.S. force of 50,000 sufficient.

Army Chief of Staff, General Eric Shinseki, cautioned that invasion and occupation of Iraq would require *several hundred thousands of troops*. Wolfowitz responded that Shinseki was *"wildly off the mark"*. Wolfowitz was a seasoned chicken hawk, who never wore a military uniform. Defense Secretary Rumsfeld, a Naval Aviator 1954-1957, studiously ignored Shinseki for the remainder of the Four Star General's tour of duty as Army Chief of Staff.

Under the able leadership of General Norman Schwarzkopf, the U. S. military, British and Coalition forces performed at their best. Airpower rapidly degraded Iraq's command and control structure. A few weeks after the ground invasion began, Saddam Hussein's Government disappeared. Bush, Cheney, Rumsfeld and Wolfowitz took a series of steps that condemned Iraq to ongoing sectarian violence. Bush and Company installed L Paul Bremer as Dictator of the Coalition Provisional Authority ("CPA").

Bremer announced the first installment of the sabotage of Iraq as a viable nation. Bremer dissolved the Iraqi Army. That meant that hundreds of Iraqi Generals and thousands of top ranking Iraqi military officers were suddenly unemployed, and henceforth would be fertile recruits for insurgency against the CPA.

Bremer's second mortal wound was to ban Ba'ath Party Members from holding high positions in government or business. The Ba'athist Party ran Iraq for thirty years. To obtain employment as a schoolteacher or at any higher job in Iraq, the candidate had to join the Ba'athist Party. Another few hundred thousand Iraqis became unemployed, and open to the lure of insurgency.

Bush and Cheney personally delivered the coup de grace to Iraq when they installed Nouri al-Maliki Prime Minister of Iraq in 2006. If Cheney was the last person Bush should have chosen as Vice President, al-Maliki was the last person Bush and Cheney should have chosen as Prime Minister of Iraq.

Historically, Iraq was never a nation state. Iraq was always three separate fiefdoms centered on Mosul in the north, Baghdad in the middle and Basra in the south. British and French politicians declared Iraq a nation, along with Czechoslovakia and Yugoslavia, after World War I. Over time, Czechoslovakia and Yugoslavia split into ethnic independent states. Iraq may suffer the same fate.

Al-Maliki lived in Iran from 1982 to 1990, when he returned to Iraq. By invading Iraq, Bush and Cheney destroyed Iraq as a counterbalance to Iran. By allowing installation of al-Maliki, a Shiite Partisan, as Prime Minister, Bush and Cheney guaranteed that Iraq would be under the influence of Iran, the leader of the world's Shiites.

Senator John McCain complains that President Obama allows al-Qaeda and ISIS to operate in Iraq and Syria. Before the nihilists' invasion of Iraq in 2003, there were no al-Qaeda or ISIS forces in Iraq. By voting for the 2003 Iraq War, McCain ensured that al-Qaeda and ISIS would come into Iraq and Syria to take advantage of the political and social instability created by the nihilists' dismantling of Iraq. For a brief time in 2006, during the Sunni Awakening, Sunni Tribal Leaders cooperated with Coalition Military to contain al-Qaeda.

When U.S. Forces left Iraq in 2011, however, al-Maliki showed his true stripes as a Shiite Partisan. Under the influence of Iran, al-Maliki began a purge of Sunni Leaders, ensuring that the Insurgency of 2005 would return with greater chaos. McCain complains that President Obama did not leave a residual force in Iraq. It was George W. Bush, however, who could not persuade al-Maliki to sign a Status of Forces Agreement in 2009. Obama pulled U.S. Military out because Iraq refused to sign a Status of Forces Agreement.

###

Would I have voted on TARP or immigration differently had I known that would cost me my senate seat? No. Because there are things far more important than being a senator. And one is to be true to your own conscience.

Former Senator Bob Bennett (R-UT)

Chapter 7
Be Far Right, Or Be Gone

Tea Party fanatics have taken over the conservative franchise. The steady move to the right has moved the center of gravity of conservatives close to the edge of the precipice. Before any vote casts in Congress, the conservative must ponder termination of his job. Will this vote result in a primary challenge by an even more conservative candidate? Bob Bennett (R-UT) was a very conservative three-term Senator from Utah. He was not primaried. He came in third in a Caucus vote that Tea Party supporters dominated in March 2010. The Caucus selected the delegates to the Convention, which in due course selected Tea Party darling, Mike Lee (R-UT).

What was Bennett's "crime"? It may have been his support of stimulus and the vote in favor of the *Troubled Asset Relief Program* ("TARP"), the bailout of the banks. Bennett voted against *Affordable Care*, and stood with conservatives on nearly all other issues. Orrin Hatch (R-UT) took note of Bennett's defeat, and survived a Tea Party challenge by packing the 2012 Caucus with Hatch supporters.

The challenge from the right means that conservatives in Congress will generally vote the default far right program, i.e., against all things Obama. Not one conservative in the House or Senate voted in favor of *Affordable Care*. Thad Cochran (R-MS) has been bringing home the bacon for Mississippi for forty years. Cochran was unable to win a majority in the June 2014 primary, and faced a run-off with Tea Party candidate, Chris McDaniel. Cochran won only by appealing for help of African American Democrats. Mitch McConnell (R-KY) easily beat off a challenge from a more conservative Matt Bevin in May 2014. McConnell's legislative agenda, proudly proclaimed in 2010, was to deny President Obama a second term.

Establishment conservatives in Utah sponsored a law, effective in 2016, that will allow candidates to go on the ballot with endorsement of voters' signatures as an alternative to selection by a nominating convention. The law is not aimed at Senator Mike Lee, but likely had in mind the fate of former Senator Bob Bennett. Tea Party fanatics railed against Governor Chris Christie (R-NJ) for putting his arm around President Obama during discussions on federal disaster funds after Super Storm Sandy struck in October 2012. Christie was a presidential hopeful in 2016, until disclosure of the scandal about his Administration's use of traffic control on the George Washington Bridge to punish the Mayor of Ft. Fee for not endorsing Christie.

Majority Leader Cantor Knocked Out

On June 10, 2014, Eric Cantor, nihilist Majority Leader in the U. S. House, lost the Virginia Primary to David Brat by a margin of eleven points. The seismic shift of the nihilists to the right is the end of compromise. Voters in Virginia's Seventh Congressional District spoke out against immigration and against Washington, DC, only a ninety minute drive north of Henrico County. Eric Cantor, as Majority Leader, spent much of his time negotiating common ground between the Tea Party and moderate conservatives. Everyone expected Cantor to replace John Boehner as Speaker of the House in the not too distant future.

Cantor, however, spent too much time on national politics and raising campaign funds for conservatives in far-flung districts. David Brat campaigned relentlessly against the confusion in U.S. immigration policy. Coincident with Brat's immigration criticism was a developing story that in 2014, sixty thousand, or more, *unaccompanied* children are expected to cross the border and enter California, Arizona and Texas, as result of political, social and economic upheaval in Guatemala, Honduras and El Salvador.

The United States government is not sending these children back, but is starting to provide housing for the initial wave in a detention center in Arizona. Governor Jan Brewer is furious. Eric Cantor appeared moderate on immigration policy. David Brat's defeat of Eric Cantor will strike terror to the hearts of all moderate conservatives. Senator Marco Rubio ran away from an immigration bill he sponsored, a year before the fall of Cantor.

On June 12, 2014, House Speaker Jon Boehner held a Press Conference. Boehner spoke briefly about Cantor's leaving the position of Majority Leader, and set June 18 for members to choose a new Majority Leader. That said, Boehner launched a broadside political attack on President Obama. According to Boehner, the President was wrong on Libya, wrong on Syria, wrong on Iraq, wrong on the economy and wrong on just about every other issue. Boehner accused the President of taking a nap on Iraq issues, and stormed off the podium. No mention of turmoil in the Republican Leadership ranks. An offensive offense is sometimes the best defense.

Boehner v. Three Billionaires

House Speaker John Boehner stubbornly refuses to bring the Senate Immigration Bill, passed in June 2013, to a vote on the House Floor. Boehner fears that the House may adopt the Senate Bill. The vote, however, would be an embarrassment. Democrats would pass the bill, with only a minority of Republican support. Nine days after Cantor's defeat, casino magnate Sheldon Adelson lobbied in *Politico* for passage of an Immigration Bill. Presumptively, Adelson sees the immigration impasse as a threat to the viability of the Republican Party. Warren Buffett and Bill Gates were so impressed that they asked Adelson to collaborate on a second immigration article.

On July 13, 2014, the three billionaires wrote in the New York Times and urged the Congress to pass an Immigration Bill. Everyone, except Speaker Boehner, wants Immigration debated. Ever the cautious shepherd, Boehner fears that the Tea Party wolves may tear his conference apart. Out of desperation, Boehner's excuse for ducking immigration is that President Obama is not enforcing the existing law. Boehner's hypocrisy culminated in a suit threatened against the President for delaying the mandate for companies to implement the *Affordable Care Act* without Congressional approval—a delay the nihilists demanded.

###

Many people consider the things which government does for them as social progress, but they consider the things government does for others as socialism.

Earl Warren

Chapter 8
Liberate Kansas!

Kansas *Captiva* is a startling concept, but one that cannot be ignored. Kansas used to be a democracy where progressives and conservatives compromised. There are insidious forces, however, that are throttling liberty in Kansas. Those forces are led by Charles Koch and David Koch, owners of Koch Industries, Inc., Wichita, Kansas. Koch Industries is a multi-billion dollar, international conglomerate and the second largest privately held Company in America, after Cargill. Koch Brothers declared war on progressive government. As industrial polluters, Koch Brothers want to destroy the U. S. Environmental Protection Agency and its local counterparts. If the Koch Brothers comply with the *Clean Air Act* and the *Clean Water Act*, Koch Industries will lose profits. Unrestrained by federal election campaign contribution limits, after Supreme Court decisions in *Citizens United v. Federal Election Commission* and *McCutcheon v. Federal Election Commission*, Koch Brothers are spending hundreds of millions of dollars to defeat progressive candidates at the ballot box in Kansas and across the Nation.

Koch Brothers and the National Rifle Association (NRA) contribute to *ALEC* (American Legislative Exchange Council) to advocate extreme or corporate friendly, anti-consumer, laws for adoption by state legislatures. *ALEC* sponsored *Stand Your Ground Laws*, adopted by two dozen states, starting with Florida in 2005.

NRA supports Stand Your Ground as one more method of increasing gun sales. ALEC sponsors use of fossil fuels, a Koch Industries cause. Governor Sam Brownback (R-KS) follows the Koch Brothers agenda in virtually all matters, except Brownback refuses to go along with Koch Brothers' opposition to subsidizing alternative energy. Brownback refuses to withdraw tax credits for wind farms. Koch Brothers do not want to see electricity produced by windmills that benefit from tax incentives, because Koch Industries owns petroleum interests.

Ever since *Buckley v. Valeo*, 424 U. S. 1 (1976), the U.S. Supreme Court has equated money with free speech—thereby subjecting laws limiting campaign spending to strict scrutiny under the First Amendment. If money equals free speech, the inability of the disaffected to influence the political process generally equates with lack of money.

The Court, as presently constituted, will allow regulation of campaign funding only to protect against corruption or the appearance of corruption. Campaign spending laws may not try to level the playing field. Inevitably, the upper one percent will choose the majority of state and federal legislators so long as the U.S. Supreme Court equates money with free speech.

Poverty lacks money for media messaging. Since the decisions of the Supreme Court depend as much on politics as on law, progressives who sit out mid-term elections lose the ability to change the right wing political bias of the Court. Senators confirm Supreme Court nominees. If nihilists pick up two more Senate seats, Congress likely will confirm no progressives to the Supreme Court.

Transformation of government by the people, for the people and of the people—to a government by and for plutocrats or oligarchs—is well under way. Kansas state legislators no longer divide between progressive and conservative. The only controversial issues Governor Brownback and Kansas legislators are willing to support in the face of Koch Brothers' objections are subjects such as tax credits for alternative energy. Koch Brothers advocate stripping unions of their power, starting with teachers and other public unions.

When Governor Scott Walker (R-WI) was subject to a Recall Election in Wisconsin in 2012, for sponsoring law to curtail bargaining rights of public employees, Koch Brothers spent millions of dollars to help Walker win the Recall Election. Koch Brothers sent their Propaganda Bus into every county in Wisconsin to "educate" the voters on the merits of restrictions on union rights.

Governor Brownback, Kansas legislators and Koch Brothers targeted Kansas teachers for restrictive laws. Kansas teachers fought back by staging a protest at the Kansas Statehouse. Governor Scott Walker (R-WI) took office in 2010, and in 2011 attacked teachers' rights and rights of public employee unions.

The People petitioned for a Recall Election. Walker won the 2012 Recall Election, supported in part by ten million dollars from the Koch Brothers. Former rising Republican star, Governor Susana Martinez (R-NM) is in trouble for going after teachers in New Mexico. The year 2010 was a watershed year for nihilists to seize control of the U. S. House and of many more state legislatures and statehouses.

Nihilists already controlled the Statehouses of each of the eleven states of the old Confederacy from Texas to Virginia, along with all but one or two state legislatures in the South. In 2010, nihilists took over northern and Midwest states. Nihilists lost no time after the 2010 decennial census, upon which seats in the U. S. House are apportioned. Nihilists drew gerrymandered districts that ensured election of nihilists, not only in the U.S. House but also in nearly thirty state legislatures. Although a minority, nihilists intend to maintain political control by using gerrymandered election districts, vote suppression and voter intimidation. In short, nihilists are converting a democratic Republic into an Oligarchy run by millionaires and billionaires.

How, you ask, can the nihilists take over in a bloodless coup in the land of the free and the home of the brave? What we are faced with is a toxic mix of propaganda, disingenuous politicians and virtually unlimited political contributions that saturate the media with nihilist propaganda.

The *Republican Noise Machine* portrays everything progressive as un-American. Rupert Murdoch, Roger Ailes and the Fox News Network, use shills like Sean Hannity to put a nihilist spin on the news. Murdoch also publishes

the Wall Street Journal, and owns Twentieth
Century Fox and Harper Collins, along with
newspapers in Britain and Australia. Murdoch
bid for Time Warner, Inc. Charles and David
Koch sponsor various right wing groups and
causes. *Americans for [Koch Brothers']
Prosperity* is a front for Koch Industries.

ALEC, the American Legislative Exchange
Council, *"is not a lobby; it is not a front group;
It is much more powerful than that"*, according to
the Center for Media and Democracy. What
motivates ALEC to distribute kits to state
legislatures with packaged draft legislation, not
only extolling the benefit of the Stand Your
Ground Law, but also proposing the text of the
law for the state legislature to adopt? The
National Rifle Association paid ALEC to lobby
for the adoption of the Stand Your Ground Law,
presumptively, as part of a program to increase
the sale of guns.

In 2005, the Florida Legislature and Governor
Jeb Bush (R) swallowed the ALEC/NRA bait.
Gun sales increased along with homicides. The
NRA was ecstatic. Stand Your Ground laws
confuse jurors on how to interpret self-defense
issues, with the result that the first person to fire
and survive is likely acquitted. Stand Your
Ground laws generally allow the defendant to
bring a motion to dismiss *before* trial.

Even where the defendant does not bring a pre-
trial motion, the jury instructions and the jurors
are confused by inclusion of stand your ground
elements. The plea of self defense is part of the
oldest body of law in Anglo American criminal

jurisprudence. Self Defense has a history of more than three hundred years based upon from tens of thousands of decided cases on every conceivable fact situation.

ALEC is dominated by corporations, which pay dues and contribute to keep ALEC alive. Not surprisingly, ALEC sponsors legislation that favors corporate interests at the expense of consumers and union members. The analysis of nihilist plans for the Nation is simple. Follow the money, watch the contributions to political campaigns and watch what governors and legislators do.

Charles and David Koch have all but killed democracy in Kansas. Governor Brownback and the Kansas legislature are virtual tools of the Koch Brothers, except for a small ray of hope coming from tax incentives granted for solar and wind projects. Governor Scott Walker started to remake Wisconsin in the nihilist mold by attacking rights of teachers and public employee union members.

Walker survived the 2012 Re-Call Election because the Koch Brothers sent their propaganda van to "educate" the voters, who soon were led to believe that a Re-Call was not the way to handle a labor dispute. November 4, 2014, will see progressive challenges to Governors Brownback (R-KS), Walker (R-WI) and Rick Scott (R-FL), among others. With hidden money supporting nihilist candidates in secret, voters are being blindsided.

Thanks to Chief Justice John Roberts and the Supreme Court's decisions in *Citizens United v.*

Federal Election Commission and *McCutcheon v. Federal Election Commission*, voters will not know what hit them. The amount of money contributed to political campaigns will be virtually unlimited, and the identity of the donors generally will hidden.

Nihilist hysteria over IRS examination of applications for tax exemption for 501(c)(4) organizations is understandable only in the context that there are other code provisions available for tax exemption: including §527 and §501(c)(3). It is contrary to law for Tea Party Groups to seek 501(c)(4) exemption for the purpose of opposing all political initiatives of President Obama.

The reason Tea Partiers want approval for a 501(c)(4) organization is that political contributors can be anonymous. It's fair enough for Koch Industries to sign an ad criticizing environmental protection. It is not fair for *Americans for Prosperity* to publish an ad against environmental protection, and not disclose Koch Industries connection. It is totally unacceptable for Koch Industries to oppose environmental protection through hidden contributions to 501(c)(4) groups.

Beware of Kochs Bearing Gifts

The City of West, Texas, suffered a catastrophe when an ammonium nitrate storage shed exploded in April 2013, killing fifteen people and taking out a middle school. Chase Koch is manager of Koch Fertilizer Division. Five months after the fertilizer explosion in the City of West, Chase donated $25,000 to the campaign of Greg Abbott, Texas Attorney General and Republican candidate for Governor. Chase's dad, Charles Koch, chipped in another $25,000 to Abbott's campaign, and Koch Industries donated another $25,000.

Texas had a long history of informing the public of the location of dangerous industrial facilities. Following the contributions from the Kochs, Texas Attorney General Greg Abbott decreed that, to protect against terrorism, the State of Texas would no longer disclose the location of dangerous industrial facilities.

Koch Fertilizer clarified that Koch contributions had nothing to do with Abbott's decision because Koch no longer stores ammonium nitrate at its Sweetwater, Texas, facility—although it used to. Koch Fertilizer contractors sometimes use Ammonium nitrate in Sweetwater for blasting purposes [?], according to Koch Fertilizer Division.

Attorney General Greg Abbott suggested that folks just drive around and ask various industrial facilities if there are any dangerous materials on site. Abbott then suggested that folks could ask the local fire departments, but it seems that the fire departments will not disclose the location of dangerous facilities if the State of Texas will not. Abbott has received another $50,000 from political action committees funded by Chevron, Dow Chemical, Lyondell and DuPont.

###

Government is not the solution to our problem.

Government is the problem.
Ronald Reagan

Chapter 9
Nihilism & Emotional Instability

On June 10, 2014, Jerad Miller and spouse, Amanda, walked into a random restaurant in Las Vegas and murdered two police officers, Alyn Beck and Igor Soldo, who were having pizza for lunch. *This is the start of a new revolution,* witnesses heard the Millers declare.

The killers pulled Officer Beck's body from the booth and covered it with a Gadsden, *Don't Tread on Me* Flag. They draped a swastika on Officer Soldo's body. The two shooters fled to a nearby Walmart, again announced their revolution, and shot a customer who tried to stop them. The revolution of two emotionally distraught antigovernment protesters was over a few minutes later, after police shot Jared Miller and Amanda took her own life. Where did the antigovernment, antipolice hatred come from? For forty years, Republicans have preached that the government is the enemy.

Ronald Reagan was crystal clear. *Government is not the solution to our problem. Government is the problem.* Nihilist candidates for office do not need a positive program to campaign on. Nihilists run solely against Washington, D. C., the seat of federal government, and win more times than not. Sarah Palin warned that federal *death panels* would kill grandma by denying healthcare, in a plot cynically hidden in the alleged federal takeover by Obamacare. Ronald

Reagan did not intend to incite unstable citizens to violence. Neither does Sarah Palin. The constant stream of nihilist anti-government propaganda, as reported and inflamed by Fox News, is pushing emotionally unstable people to launch their own violent attack on government sometimes as symbolized by police officers merely being present at any given location.

Conservative Radio Commentators broadcast anti-government tirades twenty-four hours a day. Rush Limbaugh, Laura Ingraham, Glen Beck, Sean Hannity, Michael Savage and dozens of other talk-show hosts constantly preach against the federal government and against progressive programs.

Mike Rogers (R-MI), Chair of the House Intelligence Committee, will leave Congress to become a talk show host in 2015. Ann Coulter has written half a dozen best sellers, all denouncing the federal government, liberal ideas and progressive programs. Coulter's long-term heroes are Senator Joseph McCarthy (R-WI) and Ronald Reagan. Her nemesis is Barack Obama because he occupies the Whitehouse and General George C. Marshall, because he sponsored the Marshall Plan to save Europe after the devastation of World War II.

Ronald Reagan, Sean Hannity and Ann Coulter would bristle at the suggestion that the *Republican Noise Machine* was a link in the motivation of Jerad and Amanda Miller to wantonly murder Officers Beck and Soldo in Las Vegas on June 10, 2014. What may have preceded the Millers' "revolution" likely were financial as well as emotional problems.

It is doubtful that the Millers were gainfully employed and living happy, middle-class lives. Bank Vice-Presidents seldom start revolutions. All of their lives the Millers had heard that the government is not the solution, the government is the problem. The Millers had no inner defense system to carry them through difficult times. The Millers imploded, and senselessly lashed out at two Police Officers as symbols of government that they thought somehow was trying to destroy them. The *Republican Noise Machine* claimed five more victims.

Nihilists can never be sure who will be the next victim of anti-government propaganda. On June 9, 2014, David Brat, a Tea Party Economics Professor, defeated Majority Leader Eric Cantor. On her radio show, Laura Ingraham repeatedly criticized Cantor for being too liberal on immigration. Cantor was open to the *Dream Act*, which would provide a path to citizenship to children brought to the U.S. without visas. Cantor's vulnerability came from voters' perception that he was a leader in the U. S. Government Legislative Branch. Having created a Frankenstein, nihilists are not immune from the destructive force of anti-government propaganda.

God's Messengers

Hezbollah is not the only *Party of God*. Nihilists frequently claim to be Agents of God on Earth. Some on the right are ordained ministers. Pat Robertson and Mike Huckabee preach and run for President without missing a beat. Senator

John McCain once called them Agents of Intolerance. Jerry Falwell founded the Moral Majority. Pat Robertson founded the Christian Coalition. McCain at one time felt that the Religious Right had an "evil influence" on the Republican Party.

McCain was correct, precisely because, ultimately, he felt compelled to kowtow to the Religious Right, as the gateway to the Republican nomination for President. Hat in hand, McCain dutifully delivered the commencement address in June 2006 at Falwell's Liberty University, a year before the preacher passed. The problem with mixing politics with religion is that intolerance, prejudice and oppression creep from unholy customs into the fabric of the law. Our Christian Founders embraced Slavery, and enshrined their failure in the Constitution. Christians adopted the *Fugitive Slave Act* to make sure that there was no escape from bondage.

One demonstrator against the Supreme Court's 2014 Hobby Lobby decision held a placard that summed up the modern woman's pushback against religious oppression in six short words. *Keep your theology off my biology.* Thomas Jefferson saw the need for separation of Church and State.

In his letter to the Danbury Baptists Association, Jefferson agreed that "religion is a matter ... between Man & his God" and that the First Amendment, declaring that Congress "should 'make no law respecting an establishment of religion, or prohibiting the free exercise thereof' constructed "a wall of separation between Church and State". The unholy alliance between the nihilists and the religious right seeks to remove that wall.

The Hyde Amendment, going all the way back to Representative Henry Hyde (R-IL), prohibits funds appropriated to the Department of Health and Human Services from use for abortion, except in cases of rape or incest. The Supreme Court legalized first trimester abortion in *Roe v. Wade* in 1973. The Hyde Amendment was adopted in 1976, and attached as a Rider to every annual appropriation for Health and Human Services ever since. One of the hurdles the *Affordable Care Act of 2010* was the most recent Hyde Rider, which occasioned the issuance of President Obama's Executive Order 13535 "to establish an adequate mechanism to ensure that Federal funds are not used for abortion services (except in cases of rape or incest, or when the life of the woman would be endangered)...." The hold of the religious Right on nihilist Members of Congress is so pervasive that the Obama Administration gave little thought to asking the Congress to scuttle the annual Hyde Rider. Henry Hyde was passionate about three things: prohibiting abortion, impeaching President Clinton (for fibbing under oath about a dalliance) and how unfair it was for reporters to disclose Hyde's twenty year old infidelity during the prosecution of William Jefferson Clinton for High Crimes and Misdemeanors.

Former House Speaker Newt Gingrich rejects the suggestion that he was a hypocrite for supporting the impeachment of President Clinton for having an affair at a time when Gingrich was having an affair. Gingrich denies that he did the same thing as Clinton. The difference, according to Gingrich, is that Clinton lied under oath when he denied the affair. Perjury about a dalliance apparently is a greater moral hazard that the dalliance itself.

GOP Dead End

Nihilists are taking the Republican Party to a point of no return. Extremism is a losing strategy. Republican abhorrence for President Obama has resulted in irrational and illogical opposition to programs and policies that the U.S. desperately needs.

###

"God put the Republican Party on earth to cut taxes. If they don't do that, they have no useful function."

Robert Novak

Chapter 10
GOP: Born to Protect Civil Rights

Slavery. Pat Buchanan disagreed with Novak, saying, "But, to be historically precise, the GOP was not put here to cut taxes. From infancy in the 1850s, its mission was to halt the spread of slavery. From 1850 to 1929, it was the party of high tariffs. Mission: Build the nation and protect U.S. Industry and the wages of American workers." The Battle over Slavery simmered even before the founding of our Republic. In 1833, Britain abolished slavery in the United Kingdom with the *Slavery Abolition Act*. Social and legal opinion in England turned much earlier against slavery.

Lord Mansfield went to the essence in Somersett's Case. *"The state of slavery is of such a nature that it is incapable of being introduced on any reasons, moral or political, but only by positive law.... It is so odious that nothing can be suffered to support it, but positive law. Whatever inconveniences, therefore, may follow from the decision, I cannot say this case is allowed or approved by the law of England, and therefore the black must be discharged.'* It would have been a nice touch if Lord Mansfield had written, 'James Somersett must be discharged', rather than, 'the black'.

A Customs Officer named Charles Stewart purchased Somersett in Boston, and, after transporting him to England, sought years later to ship him to Jamaica to be sold for labor, but Somersett escaped, was captured and the Chief Justice of England set him free.

Sixty years later, the U. S. Supreme Court, under the reactionary leadership of Roger B. Taney, the first Catholic on the Supreme Court, was not impressed with Lord Mansfield's decision in *Somersett*. *"The question to be raised with respect to the opinion of Lord Mansfield, therefore, is not in respect of the incongruity of the two systems but whether slavery was absolutely contrary to the law of England.* Taney reportedly was a "supple, cringing tool of Jacksonian power", who held slaves himself but set them free.

The U.S. Constitution authorized slavery, almost *sub silencio*, by counting slaves as *"three-fifths of all other persons"* for purposes of allocating Representation in Congress. The Constitution does not mention the words "slave" or "slavery".

To show the gentility of American Legislators, the *Fugitive Slave Act of 1793* referred only to "*a person held to labor*". The Act was passed under the authority of the *Full Faith and Credit Clause* of the U. S. Constitution (Art. 4, Sec. 2), which, of course, does not contain the word "slave". The *Fugitive Slave Act of 1850,* part of the *Compromise of 1850,* speaks of "*fugitives from labor*". Genteel folks know instinctively that "slavery" is a hateful term that may not be included in parlor talk or legislation.

Dred Scott was a slave in Missouri, taken to Illinois, a free state, and back to Missouri. Chief Justice Taney, not a particularly compassionate conservative, ruled that once a slave, always a slave. Taney, mischievously, went on to hold unconstitutional *The Missouri Compromise (1820),* which provided in part, "*That in all that territory ceded by France to the United States, which lies north of thirty-six degrees, thirty minutes north latitude, slavery and involuntary servitude shall be, and are hereby, forever prohibited*". Missouri, however, was excepted from the prohibition by latitude 36° 30', which forms its *southern* border, (hence the word "Compromise"), and was admitted as a slave State. Taney's invalidation of the *Missouri Compromise* likely accelerated the advent of the Civil War by making it easier for slavery to spread to new territories.

The *Kansas-Nebraska Act* (1854) allowed territories, upon joining the Union, to choose whether to permit or prohibit slavery. Senator Stephen A. Douglas (D-IL) sponsored the Act. Douglas' Bill undermined the intent of the *Missouri Compromise* by allowing local government to choose between "slave" or "free". Kansas suffered a low intensity civil war as proponents and opponents of slavery flooded in to influence the outcome of the debate, and fight over slavery or freedom. *Bleeding Kansas* is the reference that shows how violent the debate became.

GOP Birth. Out of all the turmoil over slavery, before and after the vote on the *Kansas-Nebraska Act*, the Republican Party organized. 1854 is the date given for the birth of the GOP. Horace Greeley, Samuel P. Chase and Charles Sumner provided the moral influence to organize against slavery. Greeley founded and edited the *New York Tribune*. Greeley came up with the name *Republican* in an editorial in June 1854.

"We should not care much whether those thus united (against slavery) were designated 'Whig', 'Free Democrat' or something else; though we think some simple name like 'Republican' would more fitly designate those who had united to restore the Union to its true mission of champion and promulgator of liberty rather than propagandist of slavery."

Samuel P. Chase was a Governor and Senator in Ohio for the Republican Party, which he helped organize. As an attorney, Chase represented defendants caught by the *Fugitive Slave Act*. Chase entered the race for the Republican nomination for President in 1860. William H. Seward, former Governor and Senator from New York, expected to win the Republican nomination. A local Illinois Representative in Congress, however, had the good fortune of having the Republican Convention held in Chicago in 1860. When Seward could not gather enough delegates on the first ballot, the local Illinois lad's agents started politicking to find delegates willing to switch their votes. Abraham Lincoln won the nomination.

Lincoln won the general election with less than 40% of the vote. John Quincy Adams was the only other president to win with less than 40% of the popular vote. In 1824, four candidates split the vote. Andrew Jackson won the popular vote but the House of Representatives chose Adams when none of the four candidates had a majority of the electors.

Charles Sumner was a lawyer and a U. S. Senator from Massachusetts. Originally, a *Free Soil* Democrat, Sumner, a graduate of Boston Latin School and Harvard College, was a fiery orator. Sumner denounced the *Kansas-Nebraska Act,* allowing slavery in the territories as the *Crime Against Kansas. "Not in any common lust for power did this uncommon tragedy have its origin. It is the rape of a virgin Territory, compelling it to the hateful embrace of slavery ...".*

In an effort to conciliate his Party, Lincoln chose Seward as Secretary of State and Chase as Secretary of the Treasury. But, before the 16th President could be sworn in on March 4, 1861, South Carolina seceded from the Union on December 20, 1860. President James Buchanan thought secession was illegal, but, curiously, felt the Federal Government was powerless to prevent secession.

From December 20, 1860 to March 4, 1861, seven states (later eleven) seceded to form the Confederate States of America. Buchanan's Vice President, John C. Breckinridge (D-KY), turned his back on Washington, D.C., and became Secretary of War under Jefferson Davis for the Southern States in Rebellion. Buchanan was happy to see Lincoln sworn in, so Buchanan would not have to deal with Secession.

Civil War. Lincoln and the Republicans had their finest hour. The North mobilized to save the Union and, as a byproduct, end the National Disgrace of Slavery. Most Southerners, into the twenty-first century, *still* deny that the South fought the Civil War to preserve slavery. For what reason, other than to protect slavery, would

South Carolina lead Secession *before* Lincoln took office? The South supposedly fought for independence because Northerners lacked appreciation for the Southern way of life. Free labor, however, was the overpowering monetary incentive to fight for the genteel life. The losses for both sides together in the Civil War reached about six hundred thousand.

At first, the South was successful on the battlefield under General Robert E. Lee. Lee graduated from West Point and was a Colonel in the Union Army. Lincoln offered Lee command of the Union Army to defend Washington, D. C., against the Insurrection. Lee chose to fight for Virginia and for the rebellion against his Country. Lee and many southerners had a confused vision of what citizenship in a State meant versus national citizenship. Today, it is incomprehensible that a West Point Graduate, a former Superintendent of the U. S. Military Academy and an officer in the U. S. Army would fight against his country.

The Battle of Gettysburg, July 1-3, 1863, turned the tide for the Union Army. On the last day of the battle, Major General George Pickett, under Lieutenant General James Longstreet, sent his 12,500 men up to Cemetery Ridge to attack the center of the Union Line. General Meade expected the center thrust after the Rebels failed in two flank attacks. Major General J.E.B. Stuart led a cavalry assault around the lines to try to disrupt the Union rear guard.

Brigadier General David Greg sent out the newly formed Michigan 6th Wolverines, under Brigadier General George A. Custer, to block Stuart's end run cavalry attack. After the Charge at the center failed and turned into a rout, Lee asked Pickett to reform his Division. Pickett's reply was, *"General Lee, I have no Division"*. The Civil War should have ended at Gettysburg.

General Meade, however, did not feel that the Union Army was able, after three days of battle, to chase, engage and destroy Lee's forces as they retreated towards Virginia.

Robert E. Lee and the Army of Northern Virginias fought on for another two years before surrendering at Appomattox Courthouse, Virginia, on April 9, 1865. The states in rebellion would be governed by Federal troops and Military Commanders under *Reconstruction*. Lincoln sought no vengeance against the Rebellious States, but John Wilkes Booth shot and killed Lincoln at Ford's Theater on April 14, 1865. Andrew Johnson, a Democrat from Tennessee, became President, and resisted efforts by Republican Radicals in Congress to vanquish the Southern States.

The House of Representatives impeached Johnson on February 24, 1868, for, among other things, discharging Edwin M. Stanton as Secretary of War in violation of the *Tenure of Office Act*, which passed in 1867 over Johnson's veto. The Congress reasoned that the President needed Senate approval for appointment *and* for removal of a Cabinet Secretary. The Senate (by one vote) failed to convict Johnson by the two-thirds majority required by the Constitution.

The Republicans and Northern Democrats in Congress passed and the States ratified Amendments 13, 14 and 15 to the Constitution to prohibit slavery, provide that all persons born in the United States and subject to its jurisdiction shall be citizens of the United States and of the State wherein they reside, and prohibit discrimination against voters because of race, color or previous condition of servitude. The 14th Amendment overruled Chief Justice Taney's obscene and gratuitous ruling in *Dred Scott v. Sanford* that Africans were *incapable* ever of being citizens.

The post Civil War period saw a re-alignment of the political parties. Because the Republicans championed abolition of slavery, white Southerners gravitated to the Democratic Party. Few Republicans successfully ran for office in the South from 1876 to 1960. The solid Democratic South, however, began to shatter as soon as National Democrats supported Civil Rights.

Strom Thurmond gave a hint of the realignment of political parties that was to come. In 1948, Thurmond bolted the Democratic Party to run for President as a Dixiecrat (States' Rights Democratic Party). President Harry Truman ordered desegregation of the Army in 1948. Democrats adopted a Civil Rights plank in their party platform, thereby signaling a rebirth of Civil Rights under leadership of the Democratic Party.

Strom Thurmond believed strongly then that the races should be segregated, except for his having occasional sex with his parent's colored maid (who bore Thurmond a daughter in 1925). Having the great segregationist's blood in her veins qualified Strom's child later for membership in the Daughters of the Confederacy. Thurmond moderated his segregationist stand after 1970.

Thurmond became a Republican in 1964. Reprehensible Joe (*You lie!*) Wilson (R-SC), who formerly was an employee of Thurmond, referred to Essie Mae Washington-Williams revelation, of Strom Thurmond as her father, as a "smear". After Thurmond's family confirmed the fact of paternity, Wilson apologized but maintained she should not have made the revelation in any event. There was no need to uncover all of the secrets of the genteel life.

———————

Someone had to explain the facts of political life to Dick Cheney. It was all the more telling coming from Fox News Anchor Megyn Kelly. *"Time and again, history has proven that you got it wrong as well, sir"* Cheney faltered for a moment, stumbled on Megyn's name, but quickly went back to his twisted version of events. Cheney and his daughter, Liz, blamed it all on President Obama in a Wall Street Journal Op-Ed. "Rarely has a U.S. president been so wrong about so much at the expanse of so many." Megyn Kelly faced Cheney down with the bitter truth on 6/19/14.

"You said there were no doubts that Saddam Hussein had weapons of mass destruction. You said we would be greeted as liberators. You said the Iraq insurgency was in its last throes in 2005. And you said after our intervention, extremists would have to 'rethink their strategy of Jihad'. Now with almost a trillion dollars spent there, with 4,500 American lives lost there, what do you say to those who say you were wrong about so much at the expense of so many. "—Megan Kelly

Dick Cheney has a panacea. If President Obama had maintained a sufficient military presence in Iraq, everything would work out fine. Cheney is in the last throes of trying to find a place in the sun for Liz. With dad out of office, Liz has not been able to hold a government job. After living in Virginia for 15 years, Liz decided that she was ideally suited to represent the people of Wyoming in the U.S. Senate. Liz thought that Senator Mike Enzi (R-WY) was too soft on gay marriage. In the process of slamming gay marriage, Liz and Dick turned on Mary Cheney, family member, who is married to another woman.

Liz applied for a Wyoming fishing license, and was turned down because of her Virginia residency. Liz soon gave up on her Wyoming Senate race. Liz and Dick founded a political action group, *"Alliance for a Strong America"*, a 501(c)(4) "social welfare" group organized to expose the dangerous policies of the Obama Administration. Under the Internal Revenue Code, it is questionable if the Cheneys should be allowed tax exempt status for a 501(c)(4) organization that is primarily engaged in politicking. In October 2009, Liz Cheney, Bill Kristol and Deb Burlingame founded *Keep America Safe*, another non-profit 501(c)(4) organization with a mission statement "to provide information for concerned Americans about critical national security issues".

Higher Ideals

There was a time when the Republican Party was motivated by higher ideals. Horace Greeley, Editor of the New York Tribune and a founding member, is referred to as founder of the *liberal* Republican Party—which was quite distinct from the stump that carries on today. The party was founded in 1854 to end slavery, to protect labor and to protect small farms and small businesses. John Frémont was the first Republican presidential candidate, losing to James Buchanan

(D-PA). Frémont's banner was *"free soil, free men and Frémont"*.

Abraham Lincoln was the Republican candidate for president in 1860, winning with less than forty percent of the popular vote. The Democrats splintered over slavery in 1860. Stephen Douglas ran as a northern Democrat. Buchanan's Vice President, John C. Breckinridge, ran as a southern Democrat and later served as a General and briefly as Secretary of War to Jefferson Davis and the Confederate States of America.

Before Lincoln could take the oath of office, seven southern states seceded. When Virginia later joined the rebels, Lincoln had to act decisively to keep Maryland in the Union and the capital from being surrounded by hostile territory.

###

Women would not have the problem if they did not do a certain thing.

Rush Limbaugh, blaming women for the Supreme Court's retrograde *Hobby Lobby* decision.

Chapter 11
Rape of Religious Freedom

Chief Justice John Roberts dealt the nihilists a severe blow on June 28, 2012, by upholding the *Affordable Care Act*. Conventional wisdom of Republicans expected Roberts to declare Obama Care unconstitutional. Roberts tried to make amends in 2014, but may have given nihilists a Pyrrhic victory with *Burwell, Secretary of Health and Human Services v. Hobby Lobby Stores, Inc.* When in the majority, the Chief Justice names one of the majority to write the opinion. Five unenlightened, ill-equipped men voted to protect the religious rights—not of employees—but of the employer. Roberts picked Justice Alioto to parse the paradox. Alioto had an impossible task—likely why the Chief Justice ducked the job—and Alioto failed to persuade. *Who cares if the Green Family—the owners of Hobby Lobby— have a sincere religious belief that some contraception and contraceptive means, methods, devices and pills, are contrary to the Green's religion?*

No one asked the Green Family to use contraception. The issue is not the religious sensibilities of the Green Family as owners of Hobby Lobby. Religious freedom of the employees of Hobby Lobby should not be subordinated to the sensitivities of the business owners. And no one was forcing Hobby Lobby employees to use contraception.

Since most women outside the convent rely on contraception at some point in their lives, the *Affordable Care Act* made contraception available on request as part of a woman's health care. Five unenlightened and ill-equipped men on the Supreme Court have stood personal religious freedom—protected in America for two hundred and fifty years—on its head. The majority and concurrence opinion make a mockery of personal religious freedom and a mockery of legal reasoning.

Not surprisingly, Justice Ruth Bader Ginsberg, joined by Elena Kagan, Sonia Sotomayor and Stephen Breyer, issued a dissent that amply demonstrates Alioto's hollow rationale. Alioto tried to put some limits on the scope of the majority opinion by restricting it to closely held companies. Owners of publically traded corporations do not have religious sensibilities that merit protection. How could we discern the feelings of a million General Electric shareholders? Even closely held corporations would not be heard to complain of their distaste for blood transfusions or other medical procedures (other than abortion) that are generally accepted as safe and effective and beyond religious objection. But that is the essence of the problem generated by *Hobby Lobby*.

Who is to say what sincere religious beliefs of business owners should be honored by striking down a portion of a healthcare law? Alioto tells us he would bow to science, except where women's reproductive health is concerned. Once the focus is on the owners of a business, rather than the employees, the inquiry is fatally flawed. Is it possible that Republican women do not use contraception, or are they just afraid to speak out?

The Hobby Lobby majority opinion could just as well have been written by Rush Limbaugh, who feels that conception (aside from assaults) is the result of the thing that women do willingly.

In Limbaugh's equally unenlightened view, women should just accept the consequence of their actions. Why try to gussy up a political decision with citation to legal authority, when we have Limbaugh's simplistic explanation?

There are twenty or more contraceptive methods, devices or pills available. Justice Alioto upholds the Green Family's objection to four methods as "abortifacients". Other forms of Contraception generally prevent fertilization of eggs, and, therefore, do not cause abortion. If a fertilized egg does not attach to the uterus, for whatever reason, it is equally arguable that there was no abortion. At all events, Alioto is hopelessly off the mark because he focuses on religious rights of Hobby Lobby owners to the exclusion of the rights of Hobby Lobby women employees. Alioto reasons that Government burden on religion "must serve a compelling government interest" and "must constitute the least restrictive means of serving [the government's] interest".

In other words, it would be less restrictive of the Green Family's paramount religious rights, if the Government used taxpayer funds to pay for contraceptive services for Hobby Lobby women employees. Having posed the wrong question— concerning whose religious liberty should be protected—Alioto inexorably struggles on to the wrong answer. Alioto relied upon the *Religious Freedom Restoration Act*, which was enacted in part in response to the firing of two Native Americans for using peyote for sacramental purposes. Thus, the majority joined Rush

Limbaugh in the pipedream that uninformed conservative men know better, what is good for women's health.

"The ability of women to participate equally in the economic and social life of the nations has been facilitated by their ability to control their reproductive lives." Justice Ginsberg assessed the impact of contraception, citing *Planned Parent-hood of Southeastern Pennsylvania v. Casey*. Justice Ginsberg correctly concluded that "the exercise of religion is characteristic of natural persons, not artificial legal entities".

Pact with the Devil

Ever since the days of Ronald Reagan, right wing politicians and right wing religious leaders in the U. S. have made an immoral pact, which has corrupted politics and religion. The late Jerry Falwell founded the *Moral Majority* in 1979 in protest to President Jimmy Carter's IRS denial of tax exempt status for private schools, such as Bob Jones University, (that discriminated against blacks), and to join Catholic protests against abortion.

Falwell did not accept the Supreme Court's ruling in *Brown v. Board of Education of Topeka, Kansas*. Southern religious leaders seek power from the state. Politicians seek endorsement of Southern religious leaders to win votes. Southern Democrats opposed the *Civil Rights Act of 1964* and the *Voting Rights Act of 1965*. Then there came the great migration of the nihilists from the Democratic Party to the Republican Party. Southerners continue to deny that the South fought the civil War over slavery.

Republicans deny that they joined the Republican Party because the Democrats embraced civil rights. There is racial animus evident, however, in the attitudes of the extreme right and in the Tea Party movement.

In February 2000, while campaigning against George W. Bush, Senator John McCain denounced Jerry Falwell and Pat Robertson, founder of the Christian Coalition, as Agents of Intolerance. McCain soon discovered that the easiest path to the Republican nomination was through the endorsement of the religious right. McCain emerged as a true believer by June 2006, when he delivered the commencement address at Jerry Falwell's Liberty University.

###

It kills me not to be in the White House doing what needs to be done.
Mitt Romney

Chapter 12
Can Money Buy Political Power

Romney's disappointment is the Nation's fortune. Mitt and Ann Romney claim that the news media caused Mitt Romney to lose the 2012 election. This is not true. Romney's campaign staff, aided and abetted by Willard Milton Romney and the GOP Right Wing, caused the loss. Mitt Romney is not a hard right conservative. When he was Governor of Massachusetts 2003-2007, Romney occupied the middle, rather than the right.

As the Republican Party moved further to the right, however, Romney became more isolated from the GOP Base. Romney's Staff did not concern itself with winning moderate voting blocs, so much as agonize over the possibility that the Right Wing would turn against Romney.

All Romney's staff could think about was the Base, the Base and the Base. Since the Base of the GOP represents only 30% or less of the general electorate, the math just was not there for a Romney win. Ironically, the Right Wing claims that Romney lost in 2012, and McCain in 2008, *because each failed to be conservative enough.*

According to the 2010 U. S. Census, the fastest growing voter demographic in the U. S. is the Hispanic Community. Hispanics number about 16% of the population, exceeding African Americans at 12%. Allowing for those who do not vote and for undocumented workers (who are not eligible to vote), Hispanics still constitute nearly 10% of the vote, a percentage that will increase for the next election cycles.

There may be as many as 15 million undocumented Hispanics in the U. S. Romney had a simple, do-it-yourself, Immigration Plan, which he called *"Self-Deportation"*. Romney's solution is to make life difficult by cracking down harder on employers of the undocumented. The undocumented will be unable to earn a living. Presto, the undocumented voluntarily will travel back to Mexico, Central and South America.

Romney's plan of self-deportation calculated to please the Base and not the Hispanic

Community. Self-Deportation may not have represented Romney's moderate personal feelings, but the Managers of his Campaign Staff thought it was necessary to placate the Right Wing. Ironically, many farmers and Republican business owners and managers favor a more flexible immigration policy to increase the numbers of unskilled workers available for low wage jobs.

Another example of Romney's handlers dictating defeat was Romney's minor but revealing flip-flop over the *Blunt Amendment*. Roy Blunt is a Right Wing, Christian Coalition, Republican Senator from Missouri. Congress passed the *Affordable Care Act* ("ACA") in 2010 without one Republican vote. Republicans spend most of their waking days trying to sabotage the ACA. After taking over control in 2011, Speaker John Boehner (R-OH) and the U. S. House of Reprehensibles drafted, debated and passed *50 separate bills* to repeal, defund or otherwise cripple the ACA. The Senate generally ignores the House bills to kill Affordable Care.

Roy Blunt thought up a brilliant but despicable tactic to titillate the Christian Coalition and the Right Wing, anti-Obama, fanatics. Why not pass a bill that would allow employers and health care providers to refuse healthcare based on *moral convictions* or *religious beliefs*? It would be impossible to have a *lawful, objective standard* to measure denial of healthcare based on moral convictions or religious beliefs.

Blunt ginned up an amendment to the 2012 Transportation Bill that he was certain might, if passed, cause the ACA to implode. If healthcare could be rationed according to moral conviction or religious beliefs, the ACA might be declared unconstitutional. Anyway, it would be a good Christian Coalition slap at contraceptives and abortion.

On May 1, 2012, a reporter asked Romney what he thought of the *Blunt Amendment*. Romney answered from his heart, and said emphatically that he would not support the *Blunt Amendment*. That evening, Romney's Staff again sabotaged his campaign. The Staff explained to Romney that the Base hated the ACA and that the Christian Coalition hated abortion and contraceptives, which the *Blunt Amendment* would target.

On May 2, 2012, Romney's Campaign issued a statement that he supported the *Blunt Amendment*. Romney voiced his support of the Blunt Amendment on a radio talk show. Time after time, Staff pulled Romney far to the Right, when his natural instincts were more moderate. Romney's policy gyrations, from the middle, to the right and back, made him look as though he had no core convictions. Eric Fernstrom, a Senior Romney Advisor, explained that, after the Republican Primary in 2012, it was like an *Etch-A-Sketch* game. Shake the display, and the policies that Romney solemnly announced for the Primary, fade to a blank screen. The General Election calls for new and frequently contradictory policies. All the news media did was to report the Romney flip flops. Romney's campaign sank itself, and he finally admitted as much.

Romney, of course, indulged the gyrations of his Campaign Staff. Romney's basic instinct was straightforward. Never mind the details of promoting politically correct (progressive or conservative) policies. Romney was convinced that he was a pragmatic businessperson, a problem solver, who could fix the economy. Romney still believes he was the right person for the job.

The Electorate, however, could not process the conflicting policy positions that Romney announced, abandoned and sometimes brought back. The net result was a blurred candidate. Few people, aside from Ann, knew the real Romney. Better the devil the voter was acquainted with than an unknown devil, with qualities of a chameleon. Romney's Campaign Staff sacrificed the moderate Romney to placate the Right Wing and the Christian Coalition.

Romney sabotaged his own campaign by telling his campaign donors that 47% of the people would vote for President Obama *no matter what*. According to Romney, he should not be concerned with the 47% because they would not take responsibility for their own lives. According to Romney, the 47% expected the government to provide for their needs. If Romney did not believe what he said to his donors, the public believed him. One of the workers videotaped Romney's pitch to donors. Mother Jones' David Corn released the tape to the news media.

Ironically, Romney took 47% of the vote. President Obama won re-election with 51%. In March 2013, Romney tried to distance himself from the 47% remark on *Fox News*. Romney said his remark was unfortunate and that he did not mean it. Watching the videotape from 2012, however, Romney appeared to be speaking from his heart as he addressed his donors. Maybe Romney was speaking from his pocketbook. Unlike Ross Perot in 1992, Romney did not want to spend large sums of Romney's money on his 2012 campaign.

Romney's 47% comment went viral on the internet and in the news media. The man who videotaped the remarks, however, was more disillusioned by Romney's other remarks to his donors. Scott Prouty was a bartender at the catered fundraiser. Prouty could not believe Romney's uncritical description of a factory in China that Romney wanted to buy.

The labor for the factory, working for a pittance, consisted of young girls, 18-22 years of age, who were kept 12 to small dormitory rooms, behind a barbed wire fence, with watch towers. Romney explained in his finest capitalist rationale that the fence and watch towers were not to keep the workers trapped in their jobs. Security was necessary to keep out the hordes of Chinese worker-hopefuls.

Voters could not understand Romney's refusal to release more than two years of his tax returns. Mitt's father, George Romney, released twelve years of tax returns as a presidential candidate in 1968. Mitt Romney frankly admitted that he would be subject to criticism if he released more tax returns. Romney had a Swiss bank account that he closed when exposed to public scrutiny. Romney had half a dozen deals that he personally and Bain Capital invested in the tax haven of the Cayman Islands.

Some of these investments still have to complete. Romney manipulated his 2011 tax return for public consumption to make sure he paid at least 13% tax on his income. He did this by giving up millions in charitable tax deductions. It may never be made public if Romney decides to file an amended return for 2011 to take advantage of those deductions he gave up to manipulate his tax rate (and receive a large refund) now that the 2012 election is behind him.

U. S. Chief Justice John Roberts does not seem to appreciate the threat posed to Democracy by Big Money, even as the assault is under way. We have seen Democracy overwhelmed in Kansas, Wisconsin and elsewhere by tens of millions of dollars dedicated by Charles and David Koch to undermining the political will of the electorate. Using tax deductible funds from the earnings of Koch Industries, the Koch Brothers make direct contributions to political campaigns to keep "conservatives" in public office. The Kochs are also fully engaged in a stealth crusade to skew election results by propaganda and misinformation. Who of us could suspect the bona fides of an organization the Kochs misnamed *Americans for Prosperity* (AFP)?

Truth in advertising should require the Kochs to admit that their propaganda arm is more aptly named *Americans For [Koch Brothers']* *Prosperity*. Since Koch Industries is an industrial polluter, AFP denounces the Environmental Protection Agency as un-American. Despite hiding behind organizations with innocent sounding names, the Koch Brothers logic and activities are linear and uncomplicated. Tax or regulate Koch Industries, and AFP will attack you openly or through phony organizations camouflaged in an American Flag.

When Governor Scott Walker (R-WI) was up for Recall in 2012 for undermining teachers and public employees' unions, why did the Koch Brothers come to Walker's rescue? Why would a Kansas Conglomerate take an interest in Wisconsin politics? Georgia Pacific, LLC, is a wholly owned subsidiary of Koch Industries, Inc. Georgia Pacific has six plants in Wisconsin that make tissue, paper towels and cardboard products.

Another Koch holding is Flint Hills Resources, LLC, which distributes refined petroleum through pipelines and facilities in Junction City, Waupun, Madison and Milwaukee. A Koch company distributes asphalt through terminals in Green Bay and Stevens Point. Koch Pipeline operates a 4,000 mile pipeline that crosses Wisconsin. Another Koch company supplies coal to power plants from Green Bay, Manitowoc, Ashland and Sheboygan.

The Kochs sent their propaganda bus to tour every county in Wisconsin to "educate" voters on

Scott Walker's value as Governor. The Kochs spent ten million dollars to keep Scott Walker in the Wisconsin Governor's Mansion. If the money for Walker's campaign funneled through *Americans For Prosperity*, would anyone be fooled?

The answer is yes, of course, and that would be the point of using innocent sounding names to mask a corporate polluter's objective. The Koch Brothers apparently feel that Governor Scott Walker will go easy on environmental protection, and that will increase Koch Brothers profits. Wisconsin voters have another chance to vote for Walker on November 4, 2014.

Even the Republican Party has a Propaganda Arm. Its name is Fox News Network, managed by Roger Ailes, former Republican Campaign Strategist, under the watchful eye of Rupert Murdoch. Murdoch also owns the Wall Street Journal.

Mad Hatters Tea Party

Tea Party candidates for office frequently seem to be on the lunatic fringe. Remember Sharron Angle. She was supposed to knock off Senator Harry Reid (D-NV). Sharron's strong point was that she was a Tea Party darling. Sharron's weak point was everything else. Nihilists were ecstatic because Sharron was "destined" to defeat the Democrats Senate Majority Leader. In 2011, Sharron laid out her challenge in a book entitled *Right Angle: One Woman's Journey to Reclaim the Constitution*.

Sharron joined kindred Tea Partiers, such as Raphael Cruz, Sr. and Jr., in a crusade to take "our country" back. Sharron's Senate campaign took off like a rocket. The Tea Party Express endorsed Sharron. Conservative Talk Show host Mark Levin was aboard. The Club For Growth approved. Even Joe the Plumber (Sam Wurzelbacher) joined. The Republican Mayor of Reno, Bob Cashell, however, supported Harry Reid, and dismissed Sharron as an ultra right winger.

The public knew about Sharron Angle when she ran for the U.S. Senate. She was a Member of the Nevada Assembly from 1998 to 2006. She ran unsuccessfully for the U.S. House in 2006. Sharron dodged the Press, and generally refused to take questions on her policy positions, which were extreme. Sharron claimed that Sharia Law had taken over Dearborrn, Michigan, and Frankford, Texas.

Sharron claimed that the U.S. border with Canada was the most porous border, and that the 9/11 hijackers entered the U.S. through Canada. Sharron advocated eliminating Social Security and Medicare, and leaving the United Nations. Sharron does not believe in Global Warming, and favors Second Amendment Remedies, if necessary. Harry Reid won 50.3% to Angle's 44.6%.

Then there is the case of Christine ("I am not a witch") O'Donnell, who campaigned for the Delaware Senate Seat vacated by Vice President Joe Biden, to Democrat Chris Coons by a margin of 57% to 40%.

###

*I never gave them hell. I just told the truth
and they thought it was hell.*

Harry Truman

Chapter 13
Boehner's Excuse for Nihilism

It may be the first time in the history of the United States that the Speaker of the House of Representatives refused to bring major legislation to the floor for a vote, citing as a reason that the Chief Executive allegedly failed to enforce laws previously enacted.

Boehner has been Speaker since January 2011, when the nihilists took control. The Nation never fully recovered from the Great Recession of 2008-2009, when the financial and banking system collapsed along with mortgage financing, manufacturing, autos, housing, consumer spending and most other sectors of the economy. Before leaving office,

President George W. Bush and Secretary of the Treasury Henry Paulson sponsored the Bank Bailout Bill, formerly known as the Troubled Asset Relief Program (TARP), which the 110th Congress passed under the leadership of Speaker Nancy Pelosi (D-CA).

Nihilists in Congress were not happy about TARP, and generally favored allowing the markets to work their destructive will. Nihilists thought that if a market sector was going to collapse, the government should not commit public funds to rescue a business that adopted wrong policies. When John Boehner took over as

Speaker in January 2011, the U.S. economy was still weak.

The House Calendar shows that Republicans do not see value in staying at the Capitol to address urgent legislation. The House would not be in session for a sufficient number of days to allow the House time to consider all of the important bills that the Nation needed. Immigration, infrastructure, jobs, taxation, healthcare, financial reform: the nihilists were too busy (not in the Capitol enough days) to consider important legislation.

Boehner soon realized that his excuse for doing nothing was paper thin. Boehner, after all, prepared the House Calendar. Boehner could remedy the out of town problem by scheduling more days for the members to be in the Capitol. Curiously, the House had time to bring up a bill a week, while in the Capitol, to repeal, defund or otherwise cripple the *Affordable Care Act of 2010*.

Boehner needed a new excuse for not voting on Immigration, Infrastructure or Jobs. The Senate passed a comprehensive Immigration Bill in June 2013. Unaccompanied minors showing up at the U.S. Mexican border went increased from five thousand a year in 2010 to nearly ten thousand a month by October 2013. Boehner refused to bring the Senate or any other Immigration Bill to the House floor for a vote because President Obama allegedly is not enforcing laws enacted.

Boehner's excuse is remarkable as a gambit for long term immunity for the House to do nothing until President Obama leaves office in January

2017. No House Speaker has ever made such an absurd excuse for doing nothing. Nihilists want to cancel out President Obama's eight year term in office. To be precise, Boehner wants to freeze Obama's last six years in office. Democrats controlled the House in 2009 and 2010, and passed the Affordable Care Act in 2010. If voters have had enough of nihilism, they could turn Boehner out of the Speaker's Chair on November 4, 2014. Without Boehner's leadership of nihilists, progressives could address critical legislation during the last two years of Obama's term.

Boehner and nihilists do not see the importance of addressing immigration, infrastructure, a jobs bill and a revised tax code. Governor Rick Perry ordered one thousand Texas National Guard to the border with Mexico.

What should the National Guard do at the border? Presumptively, Governor Perry does not want troops to shoot unaccompanied minors or other illegal immigrants. Most of the recent immigrants surrender immediately to the Border Patrol, so it is not clear what Governor Perry expects the National Guard to do. It looks like Perry is grandstanding for the 2016 presidential election.

Things fell apart for Speaker Boehner on July 30, 2014. New leadership in the House, occasioned by Eric Cantor's primary loss and led by Speaker Boehner, Majority Leader Kevin McCarthy (R-CA) and Whip Steve Scalise (R-LA) were forced to withdraw a border control bill that proposed $169 million to help control the border and deal with the flood of children from Central America crossing the border with Mexico.

Tea Partiers were interested only in shutting down the border to illegal immigration. Senator Raphael (Ted) Cruz, Jr, (R-TX) rallied House nihilists to mutiny against Speaker Boehner. Cruz decreed that Congress could not address border issues until reversal of President Obama's Amnesty program for undocumented children who were in the U.S. since 2011.

Senator Cruz assumed the role of House Whip, or at least Whip of House Tea Partiers. Cruz whipped House Tea Partiers previously in September 2013 in an effort to force the House to defund the Affordable Care Act or shut down the government for lack of budget approval.

Cruz also filibustered the Senate, until he was no longer able to speak. Cruz failed but the government shut down for sixteen days in October 2013, until Congress approved a budget over the objections of Senator Cruz and Tea Partiers in the House and Senate.

###

*Give a girl the right shoes, and
she can conquer the world.*

Marilyn Monroe

Chapter 14
Right Wing Conspiracy

At one point in the tumultuous Presidency of her husband, Hillary Clinton blamed their hostile opposition on a vast, Right Wing Conspiracy. Hillary, of course, was correct. The nihilist conspiracy was not well documented and exposed in the 1990s. David Brock, an apostate to the nihilist cause, deconstructed the Republican tactic of smear and disinformation in his 2004 book—*The Republican Noise Machine, Right Wing Media and How It Corrupts Democracy*. William Jefferson Clinton was President for eight years from 1993-2001.

Clinton was under official investigation for seven years. Clinton was under threat of Impeachment and in Impeachment proceedings for one year. Clinton was under attack from nihilists for all eight years. Never before in the history of the United States has a President suffered such extensive official investigations and attacks.

Clinton's offense in the eyes of Republicans was support of progressive ideas and programs. Right Wing politicians hated Clinton because he was the more skillful politician. It was inevitable that a hostile House would impeach Clinton. Former Representative Bob Barr (R-GA) filed Articles of Impeachment in 1997, *before* the Monica tapes surfaced and before Ken Starr filed his brief advocating for Impeachment.

Clinton was and is a savvy politician. He was naïve in one fateful respect. Bill Clinton actually believed that if he requested it, a Special Prosecutor would clear his name of accusations relating to the Clintons' 1978 purchase of two hundred thirty acres of Arkansas land in White Water Development Corporation, as partners with

Jim and Susan McDougal. McDougal later purchased Madison Guaranty Savings and loan, which financed some Whitewater payments and became insolvent in part because of losses due to Whitewater.

Since the Federal Deposit Insurance Corp (FDIC) insured Madison Guaranty, the federal government took over and looked for any criminal conduct in connection with Whitewater. Nihilists made Whitewater the investigation of the century. On July 20, 1993, Vince Foster, friend of the Clintons and Deputy White House Counsel committed suicide. Foster had handled Whitewater issues for the Clintons during the Campaign for president, so the nihilists spread rumors that the Clintons had Foster shot to keep him quiet.

Special Prosecutor Fiske ruled that Foster's death was a suicide. Since Attorney General Janet Reno appointed Fiske, there was a perceived conflict of interest. In August 1994, a three- judge panel on the D. C. Court of Appeals replaced Fiske with Ken Starr, former Solicitor General and federal Appeals Court Judge.

Starr re-opened the investigation into the death of Vince Foster, and, ultimately, ruled the death a suicide. Starr found no prosecutable offenses of the Clintons in connection with Whitewater. The three-judge panel expanded Starr's mandate to look into Travel Gate, whether the Clintons abused the White House Travel Agency. Starr found nothing remarkable.

Starr became bored with the job of Special Prosecutor and announced his intention to resign.

Right Wing zealots unleashed a firestorm of criticism. Starr could not resign because he had not brought Clinton down. Starr withdrew his resignation. The three-judge panel expanded Starr's "jurisdiction" to look into Bill Clinton's involvement with Monica Lewinsky, a White House Intern.

Starr prepared a brief for impeachment based upon Bill Clinton's perjury about having an affair with Lewinsky. Starr was a ferocious fighter for right wing causes, but reportedly was unavailable for military service in Viet Nam because of psoriasis. Thus, Starr joins the ranks of such celebrated chicken hawks as Rush Limbaugh, Newt Gingrich, Dick Cheney, Paul Wolfowitz and Senator Saxby Chambliss (R-GA). Shameless Chambliss defeated Senator Max Cleland (D-GA) in 2002 by running a despicable ad trying to link Cleland with Osama bin Laden. Unlike Chambliss, Cleland served in Viet Nam, leaving three limbs on the battlefield. Chambliss could not serve in the military because he had wobbly knees.

Speaker Gingrich was delighted about the Clinton Impeachment. He could get rid of a President who usually outsmarted the Congress. Gingrich arranged to have filed a Second Articles of Impeachment bill, Bob Barr's First Articles having been premature. A dedicated group of House hypocrites, including Henry Hyde (R-IL) and Bob Barr (R-GA), came over to the Senate to "manage" the Impeachment. Chief Justice Rehnquist presided at the trial. Since two-thirds of the Senate could not agree to convict on any count, the Senate acquitted President Clinton. Regular order resumed after nihilists squandered seven million dollars on trying to bring Bill Clinton down.

Conflicting Oaths of Office

Clinton was the most investigated President, but Obama is the most reviled by nihilists. That is not to say that Obama is not investigated. First, there was the minor issue of birth. Republicans wanted to disqualify Obama for allegedly being born in Kenya, Indonesia or some other foreign location. Republicans moved on to investigating alleged IRS targeting of conservative groups and Tea Party organizations seeking 501(c)(4) tax exemption.

Nihilists intend to bring down Hillary Clinton and Barack Obama with the House Select Committee on Benghazi, chaired by former prosecutor Trey Gowdy (R-SC). Republicans in Congress and state government publically swear to uphold and defend the Constitution of the United States.

There is a secret oath of office, however, that conflicts with the public oath. Republicans have sworn to destroy the presidency of Barack Obama, without regard to collateral damage caused to the Nation. Senator Mitch McConnell (R-KY), Minority Leader, at least is honest about his objective. In 2010, McConnell publically announced that his legislative agenda was to *deny President Obama a second term in office*. Despite Republican legislative opposition, Obama was re-elected in 2012.

Speaker John Boehner (R-OH) is more devious. Boehner does not admit taking the private oath of office to obstruct Obama. Boehner merely says that Obama is the worst President in history. When asked why he will not allow the House to vote on important legislation that would help with Jobs creation, Infrastructure repair and Immigration reform, Boehner offers his lame excuse. *Congress cannot pass new laws because the President allegedly will not enforce existing laws.*

According to Speaker Boehner, Congress will do nothing substantive until January 20, 2017, when President Obama leaves office. This is a stunning position for a Speaker of the House to take. It remains to be seen if the voters will allow the House to take six years off. Since the House members are elected to serve gerrymandered districts, that favor election of Republicans, there is a good chance that the nihilists will maintain control of the House indefinitely.

###

You have a Republic, if you can keep it.
Benjamin Franklin

Chapter 15
Danger From the Right

Chief Justice John Roberts has not yet admitted it publically, but there is an imperfect storm about to overwhelm the ship of state. Unlimited and unidentified contributions to political campaigns place the electorate in the position of not knowing what hit them in the lead up to elections. Millionaires and billionaires are buying politicians the way they buy businesses.

Mere lobbying of elected officials, after the election, is too remote and indirect.

Casino magnate Sheldon Adelson may spend one hundred million dollars in 2014 and 2016 to elect members of congress who will be sympathetic. Koch Brothers likely will spend more to buy a friendly Congress. Supreme Court rulings scuttled limitations on campaign financing in *Citizens United v. Federal Election Commission* and *McCutcheon v. Federal Election Commission*. Nihilists in Congress feel free to do nothing while the nation is under threat by internal and external problems.

Speaker of the House John Boehner will not even bring a substantive bill to the floor for a vote until President Obama leaves office in January 2017. On August 1, 2014, Congress planned to take a five-week break to engage in politics at home, while there are unaddressed tragedies raging at our border and with wounded veterans who have become names on a never-ending list. The Veterans of Foreign Wars issued an urgent message to Congress. Fix the veterans' health care problems with curative legislation, or do not come back from your five-week break. Voters should enforce this cure for Congress on November 4, 2014. Congress delayed their break for at least one day.

In the face of all of these threats to democracy, the main remedy in a Democracy is supposed to be the voting booth. Voters have the theoretical power to throw the entire U. S. House of Representatives and one third of the Senate out of office every two years. Theoretically, the

United States is a democratic Republic, where the voters' delegates make laws.

The Fourteenth Amendment to the U.S. Constitution defined citizenship in 1868. Our Nation prohibited slavery and guaranteed quality of political right, irrespective of race of race, by the Thirteenth and Fifteenth Amendments. Many of our basic civil rights laws enacted in the 1860s and 1870s. In the South, the post Civil War laws promoted more voting by minorities in 1872 than in 1962.

In 1876, Rutherford B. Hayes (R-OH) ended an election deadlock with Samuel J. Tilden (D-NY) by accepting the presidency in exchange for agreement to stop active federal enforcement of civil rights in the South. Civil rights languished for ninety years. Jim Crow ruled. African Americans could vote after 1876 only if they could interpret the Constitution of the United States and the Constitution of their home state to the satisfaction of voting registrars.

Civil rights started to stir again slowly and uncertainly in the late 1940s, after African Americans served their country at war for the fourth time. Polarities of the political parties inverted. Liberals founded the Republican Party in 1854 to end slavery, to protect workers and to support small business owners and small farmers.

Democrats became the champions of civil rights, which, as President Lyndon Johnson predicted, would cost the party loss of the South. In 1948, Strom Thurmond (R-SC) stormed out of the Democratic Convention. A great migration of nihilists from the Democratic Party to the formerly Grand Ole Party would follow in twenty years. Public facilities were open to all in 1964. Rand Paul (R-KY) generally supports that legislation, but is not sure the government had the right to tell Woolworth Corporation how to run their lunch counters. Political power followed the *Voting Rights Act of 1965*.

Eleven Southern States and a handful of counties, north and south, had to pre-clear with the Justice Department any proposed changes to voting places and conditions. Congress had the temerity to try to enforce the mandate of the Constitution that the Nation should be a democratic Republic where the citizens choose their government on the egalitarian concept of one vote from each citizen. The *Voting Rights Act of 1965* renewed several times, with the requirement of pre-clearance with the Justice Department maintained for changes in voting places or conditions proposed by states and counties that were prone to discriminate.

At a time when stricter and suspect voter ID measures, vote suppression and voter intimidation are sweeping the country, Chief Justice John Roberts thought this would be an ideal time to end the requirement for Southern States and some counties, north and south, to pre-clear with the Justice Department any changes proposed to voting places and conditions.

In *Shelby County, Alabama, v. Eric Holder* (2013), the Chief Justice decided that the statistics, which supported the finding of discrimination, are from the 1970s, and, therefore, are no longer reliable indicators of conditions in the twenty first century. Southern States were delighted.

The ink was barely dry on John Roberts' opinion, when stricter voter ID laws enacted in Alabama, North Carolina and Texas. The Justice Department can still bring cases of discrimination under the *Voting Rights Act of 1965*, but the pre-clearance requirement is dead until voters make changes in Congress, or until more progressives are appointed to the Supreme Court. In the meantime, cases brought by the Justice Department to enforce the voting Rights Act of 1965 will be meaningless to the extent brought after an election. There is no provision to invalidate an election or to re-do a flawed election.

Our Nation is foundering. Nihilists in Congress have paralyzed the legislative process. Thirteen million Americans are still unemployed, after the worst recession in seventy-five years. Wounded war veterans wait months for vital medical and surgical treatment. Thousands children a month are fleeing to our southern border from Guatemala, Honduras and El Salvador. *The Republican Noise Machine* is doing its best to erode the People's confidence in their Government.

American corporations are fleeing from the highest corporate tax rate in the industrialized world by merging with foreign companies and changing domicile to overseas. Nihilists have determined to destroy the Presidency of Barack

Obama, even if it means doing grievous harm to the Nation.

There is an active war in Israel and Gaza. Russia invaded Ukraine, annexed Crimea and threatens to take over eastern Ukraine. Separatists in Ukraine, armed and led by Russian officers, shot down Malaysian Flight 17 in July 2014, murdering 298 civilians. Senators John McCain, Lindsey Graham and other nihilists keep taking pot shots at the President, thereby weakening U.S. foreign policy.

In response to shelling near Ben Gurion Airport, Tel Aviv, Israel, the Federal Aviation Administration prohibited U. S. Carriers from the area for twenty-four hours. Former Mayor of New York, Michael Bloomberg, immediately flew to the banned destination on El Al Airlines.

To highlight the fractures in the Nation, 2016 presidential hopeful, Senator Raphael (Ted) Cruz, Jr (R-TX), accused President Obama of ordering the FAA to ban American Carriers from Israel as part of a conspiracy to force Israel to sue for peace with Hamas on unfavorable terms dictated by President Obama. Without any evidence, Cruz suggested that U.S. State Department pressured the FAA to ban American flights to Tel Aviv. Having conjured up a non-existent issue, Cruz offered his grandstand remedy. Cruz will filibuster all State Department appointments. Israel assured the FAA of safety measures in place, and the FAA lifted the ban.

The VFW is right. If Congress takes a five-week summer break without addressing urgent problems, including the denial of medical treatment for veterans, Congress should not bother coming back to the Capitol. If Congress refuses to address Immigration, Jobs, Infrastructure and Taxation, the voters need to elect delegates who will address the Nation's problems. House Speaker John Boehner may be content to freeze legislation until January 20, 2017, but the American people need action now.

America has one of two directions it may choose. Offer the Nation for sale to the highest bidders, such as Charles Koch, David Koch and Sheldon Adelson, or enforce reasonable limits on campaign contributions. Richard Mellon Scaife, American billionaire who targeted Bill Clinton for destruction in the 1990s, is no longer with us, having expired on July 4, 2014.

But, there are numerous other millionaires, billionaires and nihilists who threaten our democratic Republic. Elections have fateful consequences. George W. Bush gave us the 2003 Invasion and Occupation of Iraq, a neoconservative folly planned by Dick Cheney, Don Rumsfeld and Paul Wolfowitz *before* Bush took the oath of office. Forty five hundred U.S. military died. Iraq fragmented. Iran extended its hegemony in the region. The cost to U.S. taxpayers will be two trillion dollars. George W. Bush also gave us two truly conservative Supreme Court Justices, Chief Justice John Roberts and Associate Justice Samuel Alioto, who can expected to favor rights of corporations and states over individuals for the next twenty years.

State sovereignty has been a hallmark of the American Union since 1789. Until the adoption of the Fourteenth Amendment, citizenship depended primarily on relationship with a state. Even after the Fourteenth Amendment, states continued to supervise voting. Absent state citizenship, there was no ability to vote.

Residents of the District of Columbia could not vote for president until the adoption of the 23rd Amendment in 1961. State control and management of elections, whether for state or federal office, is crucial to the continued vitality of our democratic Republic. The Supreme Court must think twice before further weakening the enforcement provisions of the *Voting Rights Act of 1965*. Recent Supreme Court rulings have eviscerated laws restricting limits on campaign contributions. The impasse in Congress means that limits on campaign contributions cannot resolve without changes in the makeup of Congress.

If the American People want to claim the right to select their government, they have to step up to the responsibility. If only fifty percent of the voters show up to vote, twenty-six percent of the voters can control the Senate and the White House. Because of gerrymandered districts, a smaller minority of voters can control the U.S. House and the legislatures in the States. In the election of 2010, Democratic candidates in the U.S. House won a majority of the votes cast. Republicans took control of the House because of gerrymandered districts. The Nation is entering a dangerous time for Democracy. Our Supreme

Court has put the country up for sale to the highest bidder by gutting limits on campaign contributions.

The Supreme Court has given the green light to states to discriminate by invalidating pre-clearance requirements of the *Voting Rights Act of 1965*. A minority of nihilists has taken over the House of Representatives and state legislatures through gerrymandered election districts. The former majority of white citizens panicked over loss of political control to burgeoning minorities, who have become the new majority in population. There is a conspiracy, led by states' rights activists and white supremacists with the blessing of the U.S. Supreme Court, to suppress votes and intimidate voters in a desperate attempt to avoid a democratic vote count.

Nihilists want to revise the Fourteenth Amendment, which extends citizenship to all persons born in the United States and subject to its jurisdiction. Population numbers inexorably show that minorities are the new majority. Republicans want to look to pedigree to change the numbers. Nihilists want to examine the place of birth of the parents of dubious residents.

If the parents of the person claiming citizenship are not citizens, nihilists want to cut off citizenship of the children. It was easy for nihilists to challenge the legitimacy of Barack Obama, whose father was Kenyan. Birthers never spoke the words, but they do not accept the Fourteenth Amendment's precept that birth on American soil brings citizenship. If the nihilists

144

prevail, the United States will no longer be a democratic Republic where the electorate chooses the government based upon one person having one vote.

If the nihilists prevail, the United States will have a permanent underclass to wash our laundry at subsistence wages. If one of the underclass strays near a polling place, Republican National Committee Chair Reince Priebus will be there with a challenge: *You are not a citizen, and you certainly do not look American.*

There are two *Dream Acts* and two different visions. Progressives want to extend citizenship to children who accompanied their parents without visas. Nihilists have a dream to throw the undocumented out in a desperate effort to roll back the population clock to a kinder, whiter time. Of course, the South did not fight the Civil War to preserve slavery. Southerners fought to preserve gentility and States Rights and to resist federalism and northern insensitivities.

May be the South did not lose the Civil War. They control the House of Representatives, and with their allies, may take control of the Senate. Perhaps it is time for the rest of us to relax, to sip a mint julep, sit back and enjoy life while our twenty first century slaves, created by the distinction between citizens and residents, do the dirty work

If the Koch Brothers can buy the Governors of Kansas, Wisconsin, and Florida, who are we to resist. If the Kochs can install their own Senator in Oregon, is that not free speech at work? If the Koch Brothers can defy the IRS by claiming

501(c)(6) tax exemption for *Freedom Partners*, why can the Kochs not spend their own money as they see fit? If *Freedom Partners* masquerades as a *Chamber of Commerce,* should we allow the IRS to curtail free speech by investigating what in essence is the Koch Brothers' Bank?

In the words of Quintus, Lieutenant to Maximus, General of the Northern Armies of Emperor Marcus Aurelius—*A People Should Know When They Are Conquered.* Herman Cain was a motivational speaker for *Americans For* [Koch Brothers'] *Prosperity* in 2012. Koch Brothers sent their motivational speaker to be the Republican candidate for President.

Nihilists chose a competing billionaire, Mitt Romney. The People re-elected Barack Obama. Let us see who controls the Congress in January 2015, and who the Koch Brothers offer as Chief Executive in 2016. May be we are not a conquered people, if we have the will to vote.

###

Round up the usual suspects.
Claude Raines, Casablanca

Chapter 16
The Lineup for 2016

Republicans face structural challenges in presenting candidates for the 2016 presidential campaign. How can the GOP offer the Koch Brothers' candidate as the voice of the people? Propaganda is a powerful persuader. The Big Lie is most effective when a government can convince media to affirm the message. Fox News, the propaganda arm of the Republican Party, is at the ready to explore the conservative side of the news. The U.S. House of Reprehensibles declared war on democracy in 2011.

As the result of gerrymandering, the People's House represents a distorted and overweighted segment of the electorate. If voters allow it, Speaker Boehner will continue to bottle up most meaningful legislation until President Obama leaves office in January 2017. Progressives hold the White House and the Senate. The Senate, however, strains to be progressive as result of arcane rules that generally require sixty percent of its members to advance legislation to a floor vote. All political parties have to run a slanted campaign in primaries to placate the base, and run in the other direction toward the middle in the general election. Ultraconservatives, however, have moved the GOP so far to the extreme right that coming back to the middle is an impossible task.

In 2012, all the King's horses and all the King's men could not put Mitt Romney back together again. It is a virtual contradiction in terms for a GOP candidate to have the blessing of the base in the primary and be acceptable to the broad middle band of voters in the general election. Republicans must present two irreconcilable personas to run the gauntlet. Despite serving as a moderate Republican Governor of Massachusetts, Mitt Romney could not escape the antidemocratic implication of the endorsement of the upper one percent.

Republicans have the opportunity of a lifetime in 2016. Gerrymandered Districts may allow the GOP to hold the House of Reprehensibles and the legislatures in thirty states. The Senate may go Republican depending on the outcome of six closely contested States. All the Koch Brothers and Sheldon Adelson have to do is to flog a billion dollars from the one percent to elect a Republican president. If the GOP can capture all three branches of government, Republicans can tell the Big Lie with effect. Rupert Murdoch and Roger Ailes will broadcast the Big Lie through Fox News, the Wall Street Journal, the New York Post, News Corp, Twenty First Century Fox and Harper Collins Books.

Remember the horror of the propaganda war the U.S. Government waged against the American People in the run up to the 2003 Invasion of Iraq. George W. Bush, Dick Cheney, Don Rumsfeld and Condi Rice all warned that, *We do not want the first sign of WMD in Iraq to be a mushroom cloud.* CIA analysts and the scientific community saw no evidence of WMD in Iraq in 2002. Cheney and Scooter Libby drove to Langley, Virginia, multiple times to tell CIA analysts to "find" WMD in Iraq.

The Bush Administration sabotaged the CIA, which is dedicated to finding facts. Fox News supported the war propaganda. Progressive Presidential hopefuls and Senators John Kerry, Hillary Clinton, Joe Biden, Joe Lieberman voted for war. Barack Obama, a member of the Illinois State Senate, came out against "dumb wars". If the Republicans take the Senate in 2014 and the White House in 2016, the GOP and Fox News can tell the Big Lie for the next eight years.

The GOP line up for 2016 may be a Line Up. Chris Christie, Governor of New Jersey, is under investigation by two U. S. Attorneys for bridge scandals. Rick Perry, Governor of Texas, is indicted for abuse of power by threatening and cutting off funds to force a District Attorney (who happened to be a Democrat) to resign after a DWI conviction.

Bob McDonnell, former Governor of Virginia, may not be the best VP pick after his trial for corruption and bribery. From his credentials, McDonnell is the perfect GOP candidate. Mitt Romney had to think long and hard in choosing Paul Ryan over McDonnell for Vice President. McDonnell was a Lt. Colonel in the Army Reserve, and served as a medical supply officer at Army clinics in Germany and Newport News, Virginia.

He served in the Virginia House of Delegates from 1992 to 2006, and was Attorney General of Virginia. McDonnell graduated from Notre Dame on an ROTC scholarship. He was awarded an M.A./J.D. Degree in law and public policy by Christian Broadcasting Network University (now, Regent University).

McDonnell's Master's Thesis supported and was entitled *The Republican Party's Vision for the Family*. At his corruption trial, McDonnell coolly blamed it all on his wife. Floating a bawdy defense that may precipitate a post trial divorce, McDonnell complained that all those gifts that were thrust upon him by a Virginia businessman were the result of his wife's fling with the benefactor. Known as *Governor Ultrasound* for signing a bill to require a scan before an abortion, McDonnell made one last assault on his wife's honor by alleging her infidelity for his acceptance of bribes.

On 9/4/14, a jury in Richmond, Virginia, found McDonnell and his wife guilty on multiple counts of conspiracy and bribery. Sentencing is set for January 2015. The McDonnells will file an appeal. Governor Ultrasound found himself on the wrong end of a probe.

Other Republicans in line for 2016 include Mitt Romney, Paul Ryan, Raphael (Ted) Cruz, Jr., Newt Gingrich, Rand Paul, Rick Santorum, Bobby Jindal and Marco Rubio. Romney and Ryan met at Chicago's Union Club on August 21, 2014, and each essentially said, *After You*, for the 2016 campaign. Romney still thinks he is God's (and possibly the Koch Brothers') answer to today's problems.

Ryan memorialized his perennial Budget for 2011-2015 in a book called *The Way Forward: Renewing the American Idea.* The only problem with Ryan is that he is another Republican who would like to privatize Social Security, reduce Medicare to a Voucher program, repeal the Affordable Care Act and balance the federal budget on the backs of the poor and the middle class. Newt Gingrich still cannot explain why he needed a $500,000 revolving credit at Tiffany's to keep Callista in baubles (as if that were any of our business).

Rick Perry is outraged that on 8/28/14 (while Congress was on a five week vacation), President Obama admitted to not having a fully developed policy on use of air power in Iraq and Syria to counter ISIS (referred to as ISIL by the Obama Administration). In 2013, President Obama requested authorization from Congress to use air power in Syria against Bashar al Assad. Speaker Boehner never brought the request for a vote.

Rubio was co-sponsor of the Senate Immigration Bill in 2013. After the xenophobes in the GOP base signaled mutiny, Rubio voted against his own Immigration Bill. Having lost Hispanic support by abandoning immigration reform, Rubio can rest assured that most Miami Cubans over the age of 78 will automatically vote the GOP ticket in ongoing protest to JFK's withdrawal of U.S. air support for the Bay of Pigs Invasion of Cuba in 1961.

Rick Santorum can campaign on divisive social issues. If Bob McDonnell escapes conviction, a Santorum-McDonnell ticket would cover all the social issues and might win support of the Christian Coalition. Raphael (Ted) Cruz, Jr., may not think God sent him here to be president, but Raphael (Ted) Cruz, Sr., certainly does think God supports the GOP and Ted, Jr.

Cruz could make for an interesting presidency. Imagine, if Joe McCarthy ran for president in 1954. Michele Bachmann is waiting for a message from God before announcing her 2016 campaign. Bachmann blamed her Iowa campaign manager for selling out to the Ron Paul Campaign in 2012 for a bribe. Turns out that

Michele was right. On 8/29/14, Jesse Benton resigned as campaign manager for Senate Minority Leader, Mitch McConnell.

Benton managed Ron Paul's 2012 presidential campaign and Rand Paul's 2010 Senate campaign. On 8/27/14, Kent Sorenson (former Iowa State Senator) pled guilty to accepting a $73,000 bribe to switch support from Michele Bachmann to Ron Paul. Benton proclaimed his innocence in the Sorenson bribe.

Former Florida Governor Jeb Bush may have waited too long to make up his mind to run for president. Rand Paul presents a curious mix of conservatism and libertarianism. When Kentucky Senator Rand Paul teams up with New Jersey Senator Cory Booker to level the playing field for African Americans, Paul shines up like a Democrat. Libertarians, however, may be more dangerous than are Republicans.

Libertarians do not believe in government. Paul is a Tea Party favorite. Paul supported FreedomWorks in its lawsuit against the NSA for surveillance of communications' metadata. Like his father, Rand Paul opposes the Federal Reserve Bank and has threatened with hold up nominees unless the Congress agrees to an audit of the Federal Reserve. Unlike his father, Rand Paul believes in controlled use of U.S. power abroad, but considers the 2003 Invasion of Iraq was not proper use of U.S. Military.

###
Bibliography

American Prometheus, The Triumph and Tragedy of J. Robert Oppenheimer, by Kai Bird and Martin J. Sherwin, Vintage Books (Random House), soft cover (2006).

The Benghazi Hoax, CreateSpace (Amazon), paperback & e-book (2013) by David Brock

Fiasco: The American Military Adventure in Iraq, Penguin Press (2006) by Thomas E. Ricks

Free Soil, Free Labor, Free Men: The Ideology of the Republican Party before the Civil War, Oxford University Press (New York 1995 paperback) by Eric Foner

Game Change, Obama and the Clintons, McCain and Palin, and the Race of a Lifetime, Harper Collins (2010), by John Heilemann and Mark Halperin

Going Rogue, An American Life, Harper Collins (2009) by Sarah Palin

Hard Choices, Simon & Schuster (2014) by Hillary Rodham Clinton

Imperial Life in the Emerald City: Inside Iraq's Green Zone, Vintage Books (2006) by Rajiv Chandrasekaran

Path to Prosperity, House of Representatives Budget for Fiscal Years 2012-2015

Republican Noise Machine, Right Wing Media and How it Corrupts Democracy, Random House (2004) by David Brock

Right Angle: One Woman's Journey to Reclaim the Constitution (2011)

Rise of the Vulcans: The History of Bush's War Cabinet, Viking Penguin (2004) by James Mann.

Takeover: The One Hundred Year War for the Soul of the GOP and How Conservatives Can Finally Win it, WND (WorldNetDaily) Books (2014), by Richard Viguerie

Too Big to Fail, Andrew Ross Sorkin

##

Notes

Preface. As of 2013, the largest privately held U. S. Company is Cargill, with revenues of $136 billion and 140,000 employees. Koch Industries has sales of $115 billion and 60,000 employees. Forbes,com/list of largest private companies in the U.S. David Koch was Vice Presidential candidate for the Libertarian Party in 1980.

In 1974, Charles Koch Foundation founded the Cato Institute, a libertarian think tank, and an Internal Revenue Code § 501(c)(3) group. Books by the Cato Institute include *In Defense of Global Capitalism* and *Restoring the Lost Constitution*. Cato Institute believes in

Downsizing the Federal Government. Koch Brothers contribute more than 51% of operating money for Cato Institute.

Koch Brothers filed suit in 2012 for control of Cato Institute. *Kochs Launch Court Fight Over Cato*, Politico, 3/1/12, by Mike Allen. The Koch Brothers believe that the battle over America will be a war of ideas and propaganda. To win that battle, the Kochs want to control or have influence over the Cato Institute, *Alec*, *FreedomWorks*, and *Freedom Partners*. Kochs' propaganda arm is *Americans For* [Koch Brothers'] *Prosperity*. Voters are mere pawns on the Koch Brothers political chessboard.

Sharron Angle ran against Harry Reid in 2010. Angle is a Tea Party favorite, who has the support of the Koch Brothers. Angle hosts a right wing radio show, and has suggested that Harry Reid is mentally challenged with his fixation on the Koch Brothers. *Conservative Commandos* (Radio Show) 4/3/14. Harry Reid's criticism of the Koch Brothers from the Senate Floor is a protest against big money funding extremists' campaigns. Republicans do not own the First Amendment.

Chapter 1, Hot Button Issues.

Taking Back the U.S. Raphael Cruz, Sr., left Cuba in 1957 for a better life in the U.S, and is, of course, the father of Senator Raphael (Ted) Cruz, Jr (R-TX). The clarion call *"to take the country back"* is the mantra of the Tea Party. Raphael Cruz, Sr., sees American Exceptionalism from the viewpoint of rugged individualism, an entrepreneurial America freed of government regulation.

The prototypical Republican is an independent businessperson, who craves smaller government and lower taxes. Former Majority Leader (2003-2005) Tom Delay (R-TX) was the model Republican. DeLay owned his own exterminating company before election to the Texas House and then the U.S. House. Known as *the Hammer*, Delay assisted Newt Gingrich in the Republican takeover of the House after forty years in the minority.

A staunch conservative, Delay moved up as whip and then Majority Leader. The conservative mantra echoed by Cruz, Sr, Delay and Tea Party zealots, is similar to that praised by Charles and David Koch, billionaire owners of Koch Industries. The war on government is a war on taxation. Fear of redistribution of wealth motivates dismantling government, reducing government services for the less fortunate and lowering taxes.

Voter Turnout. The Presidential elections of 2012, 2008, 2004 and 2000 all had more than fifty percent of registered voters turn out to vote. The mid-term elections (no president on the ballot) of 2010, 2006, 2002 and 1998 had voter turnout near thirty-seven percent. Infoplease.com, National Voter Turnout in Federal Elections: 1960-2012. The lack of voter participation in mid-term elections makes it easier for an organized minority to seize control of the U.S. House, especially where the party in power in state legislatures has drawn gerrymandered election districts that allow minority representation to prevail over the will of the people.

Immigration. Children who are nationals of Canada or Mexico and enter the U.S. illegally may be sent back summarily. Children who are nationals of non-contiguous countries must be taken into custody, protected and given a deportation hearing. 8 USC § 1232. Department of Health and Human Services (DHS) tries to find a relative in the U.S. to shelter the child. If there is no relative, DHS will provide shelter and act as parent.

Arrival of five thousand mostly unaccompanied children a month at the U.S.-Mexico border from Guatemala, Honduras and Salvador is testimony that the word on the street is that the U.S. will grant asylum to illegal child migrants. The situation is so serious that Vice President Biden visited Central American Governments in June 2014 to urge restraint. Secretary of State John Kerry is also scheduled to visit Central America to see if there is a reasonable way to stem the flow of illegal child migrants.

Vote by Mail. Oregon adopted all mail voting after a referendum in 1998. Colorado and Washington State followed. California, Arizona, Montana, Hawaii, Utah and New Jersey are considering all mail voting. States with all mail voting have increased voter turnout. For 2012, U.S, turnout was 58.7%; Colorado 71%; Washington 65%; and Oregon 64.3%. IVN.com.

Bill Sizemore, former Republican Governor of Oregon, sees vote by mail as rife with fraud. *Vote by Mail, a Formula for Fraud*, Bill Sizemore, April 8, 2013, NewsWithViews.com.

"For a rapidly increasing number of Americans, voting at the precinct place on election day is a historical relic." *Ballot Integrity and Voting By Mail: The Oregon Experience*, report dated June 15, 2005, by Dr. Paul Gronke, Early Voting Information Center, Reed College, Portland, OR. Dr. Gronke concludes that VBM (Vote by Mail) is generally more accurate.

Voter fraud is not restricted to the huddled masses. Clackamas County indicted a Republican election official in for writing in the names of Republican Candidates on ballots left blank for those positions. BradBlog.com, 11/2/2012, updated 11/2/12. Sourced on Willamette Week and Portland Tribune. cf. *Oregon Election Worker, Fired*, Huffington Post, 11/6/12, by Daniel Lippman.

Chapter 2, Benghazi.

Witch Hunts. Lewis Strauss agreed to accept President Eisenhower's nomination to Chair the AEC only on condition that J. Robert Oppenheimer have no further connection with the AEC. Oppenheimer was qualified to be the Scientific Director of the Manhattan Project that developed the Atomic Bomb in the 1940s.

When he was not needed in 1953, Oppenheimer was cast aside as a security risk. Strauss feared Oppenheimer's superior talent as a physicist and ability to dominate any meeting. *See,* generally, *American Prometheus, The Triumph and Tragedy of J. Robert Oppenheimer,* by Kai Bird and Martin J. Sherwin.

Oppenheimer's downfall came in 1944-45, and beyond, when he opposed the development of the hydrogen bomb. Edward Teller, a member of Oppenheimer's nuclear weapons development team at Los Alamos Lab, NM, was fixated on development of the H-Bomb. Before the fission bomb could be ready for battlefield use, Oppenheimer opposed diverting scarce resources to development of the fusion bomb. After fission bombs destroyed Hiroshima and Nagasaki, Oppenheimer opposed development of the H-Bomb on policy grounds.

Since his main preoccupation in life was the development of the H-Bomb, Teller viewed Oppenheimer as an implacable enemy. U. S. Air Force leaders favored development of the H-Bomb, as did Lewis Strauss, who did not want to hear Oppenheimer's voice in nuclear matters. There would be no further debate because, without a security clearance, Oppenheimer could not sit at the table. Strauss' letter, stripping Oppenheimer of his secret clearance, objected to Oppenheimer's past associations *and his policy positions.* It was a threat to national security to disagree with Strauss on policy.

Senator Joseph McCarthy's tactics still influence Washington politics. Witch Hunts and smears are still in use. Senator Ted Cruz (R-TX) gives all the appearances of following in McCarthy's footsteps. During the Senate Hearing on confirmation of Chuck Hagel as Secretary of Defense, Cruz tried to smear Hagel because the public does not know who contributed to Hagel's Senate campaign.

Cruz suggested, without any proof, that foreign governments possibly contributed to Hagel's Senate campaigns or paid for his speaking fees. Hagel's political offense was that he did not support John McCain for president in 2008. Hagel's wife campaigned openly for Barack Obama.

Four Dead Americans. U.S. Special Forces arrested one of the attackers of the Benghazi Consulate, Ahmad Abu Khattallah, around June 14, 2014, but there are still details of the attack to be uncovered. If the Select Committee can find facts in a nonpartisan inquiry, the hearings could benefit State Department security.

Pat Smith, mother of slain State Department official Sean Smith, appeared on CNN with Jake Tapper June 16, 2014, and blamed Hillary Clinton for her son's death. Mrs. Smith had not yet heard from Hillary Clinton or President Obama, and wants answers as to why her son died. No one will be able to give a satisfactory answer.

Nihilists such as Lindsey Graham and John McCain want Khattallah sent to Guantánamo

Prison for interrogation and, eventually, trial by a military commission. President Obama will have Khattallah tried in a U.S. District Court, where hundreds of terrorists have been tried and convicted.

Trey Gowdy (R-SC), Chair of the Select Committee on Ben Ghazi, will have to walk a fine line between finding Hillary Clinton guilty of something and honoring due process. If Gowdy errs on the side of fairness, he will lose his status as a Tea Party darling. The Club for Growth awarded Gowdy as *Defender of Economic Freedom*.

Showmanship. The announcement of the Select Committee on Benghazi has some nihilists on edge. Darrell Issa saw the spotlight redirected from his investigation in the House Oversight Committee to Trey Gowdy's Select Committee. Desperate to maintain his place in the sun, Issa promptly threatened to subpoena Secretary of State John Kerry to testify.

Kerry, of course, has no connection with Benghazi, but does have control over State Department personnel and historical records. Congressman Elijah Cummings, who is ranking minority member on both Committees, will be busy trying to keep both investigations honest. Issa may defer to the Select Committee on bringing Kerry on camera.

Tax-Exempt Status. The law under Internal Revenue Code § 501(c)(4) allows tax exemption only if the organization claiming the exemption is engaged *exclusively* in social welfare. The IRS issued an interpretation in 1969, however, that provided tax exemption if the organization was engaged *primarily* in social welfare. Tea Party zealots are hysterical that Lois Lerner, IRS Official charged with approving tax-exempt organizations, was persecuting Tea Party groups by reviewing their activities before granting tax exemption.

The IRS, however, must determine the nature of a group's activities to determine if the activities are *primarily* for social welfare. Ironically, the Obama Administration is reluctant to enforce the law as written for fear that the IRS will be forced to deny tax exemption to virtually all Tea Party organizations, who, after all, are engaged in politicking and (as the law is written) are not qualified under 501(c)(4) for tax exemption.

The IRS generally did not deny Tea Party applicants tax exemption under 501(c)(4) for reason of political activism. Tea Party hysteria over IRS review of Tea Party activities (pursuant to application for tax exemption) is nothing more than a Tempest in a Tea Pot. IRS officials should enforce the law as written. The sole reason for 501(c)(4) tax exemption was that the activity of the organization would be for social welfare purposes, and not for politicking.

Lawrence O'Donnell, host of his CNBC show, disclosed the absurdity of the furor over 501(c)(4) tax exempt status. If an organization is engaged in politics, and wants tax-exempt status, there are other tax code provisions that allow tax exemption for politicking. For example, 501(c)(3) or 527. Why the hysteria over 501(c)(4)? Republicans fear disclosure of names of campaign contributors. Organizations that qualify under 501(c)(3) or 527 must disclose the identity and amounts of the contributions.

Organizations that qualify under 501(c)(4) can and do keep all donors names secret. That is why savvy political operatives like Karl Rove maintain a stable of separate fundraising organizations under various sections of the Internal Revenue Code. *American Crossroads* is tax exempt as a Super Political Action Committee under section 527.

Crossroads GPS is tax exempt under 501(c)(4). Rove keeps donors' names secret. *Dark Money*, i. e., anonymous money, is mugging the American People, and the U. S. Supreme Court is an unindicted co-conspirator. Chief Justice John Roberts provided the get-away car with Justice Anthony Kennedy at the wheel. *Citizens United v. Federal Election Commission* (2010) 558 U.S. 310

Koch Brothers would appear to be in violation of the law by using 501(c)(6) organizations, such as *Freedom Partners*, to funnel dark money to other nihilist groups to affect the outcome of elections. CREW, *Citizens for Responsibility and Ethics in Washington*, sued Freedom Partners for disclosure of amounts of contributions. CREW Blog dated 11/8/13.

To complete the charade, *Freedom Partners* formal name is *Freedom Partners Chamber of Commerce*. The Center for Media and Democracy, Source Watch, *Freedom Partners*. Describing itself as a "nonprofit, nonpartisan 501(c)(6) Chamber of Commerce, Freedom Partners operates as Koch Brothers secret bank. Mike Allen and Jim Vandehei, *The Koch Brothers' Secret Bank*, Politico, 9/11/13.

Health Care. It is nothing short of stunning that nihilists monolithically and intractably opposed the *Affordable Care Act* from 2009 until millions of Americans gave approval in 2014 by purchasing health insurance under the Act. President Nixon advocated an employer-based national health care regime with an individual mandate in 1973. The Heritage Foundation, a conservative think-tank, extolled the merits of a national health care law with an individual mandate in the 1990s.

Everyone has to participate to keep health care affordable. In 2006 Governor Mitt Romney (R-MA) instituted a state health care plan with an individual mandate in Massachusetts. All praise to Romney for *avant-garde* social policy. Romney wrote an Op Ed in the New York Times recommending that his health care law be the model for a federal health care law with an individual mandate.

Romney relied upon MIT Professor Jonathon Gruber to consult on development of the Massachusetts health care law. President Barack

Obama retained Professor Gruber as a consultant for the development of a national health care law with an individual mandate.

President Obama and progressives in Congress passed the *Affordable Care Act* in 2010 with an individual mandate, and established minimum health care insurance coverage standards. Not one nihilist voted for *Affordable Care*. As soon as President Obama touched national health care, the nihilists opposed national health care.

Professor Gruber is on record as saying that, *There is no f'ing difference between Romney Care and Obama Care. The nihilists' bailout on national health care is the most remarkable and unprincipled volt face in the political history of the U.S.*

The blind opposition of nihilists to everything Obama is understandable only by their willingness to harm the American people, so long as nihilists can deny President Obama a legacy. Ironically, despite all the hysteria from conservatives, there is no such thing as Obama Care as a government health insurance plan for sale to the public.

The *Affordable Care Act* established minimum standards for *private* health care insurance plans. The federal government does pay for Veteran's Care, Medicare and Medicaid, but private companies underwrite the remainder of the healthcare insurance market. It is curious to hear nihilist-infected seniors rant that they do not want the government messing with Medicare, for which, of course, the federal government pays.

Bergdahls. The trashing of Bowe Bergdahl and his parents by the nihilists was shocking. The father was portrayed as a Taliban because he grew a beard and learned Pashto to try to persuade the Taliban to release his son. The frenzy reached a climax when it was disclosed that Bergdahl previously joined the U.S. Coast Guard, and was separated a month after joining. If the Bergdahls, as a family, could be labeled bad, then the exchange of Taliban prisoners would be bad. Nihilists failed to realize that the exchange of prisoners was necessary at the end of the war. In nihilists' eyes, the war is perpetual. Guantánamo forever.

Chapter 3, One Citizen, One Vote?

Grass Roots Battle. There is a ferocious struggle in the Courts to keep the playing field level. Republicans have turned against early voting, presumptively because early voting tends to increase the vote count, which favors election of Democrats.

In 2012, Congresswoman Corrine Brown sued Florida Secretary of State Ken Detzner, Case No 3:12-cv-852, to strike down a 2011 Florida statute, F.S. 101.657(1)(d) that reduced the number of early voting days. Judge Timothy J. Corrigan, U.S. District Court, Jacksonville., FL, denied an injunction, by order dated 9/24/12, because plaintiffs failed to show "intent to discriminate against minority voters, or that Florida's current Early Voting Statute operates to deny or abridge African Americans right to vote on account of their race".

In *State of Florida v. Sergio Robaina*, Case No F12-20015, 11th Circuit, Miami-Dade County, Judge Milton Hirsch, on 1/23/13, refused to dismiss charges that defendant was in possession of multiple, completed, absentee ballots as a "ballot broker" on the defense that defendant was facilitating the rights of others to vote and, therefore, that the prosecution was unconstitutional. Robaina initially was charged with two felony counts, later reduced to misdemeanors, under a 2011 County Ordinance designed to stop ballot brokering.

Mr. Robaina, who was seventy-five years of age at the time, denies that he tried to influence voting, but only tried to assist others, many of whom were elderly or ill, to have their ballots delivered. Miami-Dade County Ordinance 12-14, under which Mr. Robaina was charged, makes it unlawful to have in possession more than two absentee ballots unless ballots of immediate family members.

On December 19, 2012, the Miami-Dade County Grand Jury filed a Final Report on Voting, Voter Fraud and Absentee Ballots. Prior to 1997, Florida law allowed absentee voting only for cause. After 1997, absentee voting could be for convenience. In the 2000 election, absentee ballots counted for seven percent of registered voters. By 2012, absentee ballots amounted to twenty seven percent of registered voters.

The Grand Jury noted (1) risk of fraud in absentee ballots and (2) even longer lines to vote if the twenty seven percent of absentee voters voted in person. The Grand Jury recommended increased Early Voting Time, stricter controls on absentee ballots and adjusting precincts so that time required to vote in one would be comparable to other precincts.

In person voter fraud in the U.S. is a rarity. Voting by absentee ballot presents opportunities for fraud on many levels. It is interesting to note that the State of Oregon employs voting *by mail only* (without allowing voting at polling precincts) in general elections without reports of widespread fraud. In 2000, Oregon conducted a presidential election entirely by mail, *with an eighty percent participation rate.*

Cherokee Betrayal. It is not expected that nineteenth century land speculators in the State of Georgia would have compassion for Native Americans. Since the Georgia legislature at the time was subject to the lure of lobbyists and land speculators, it is not surprising that the State of Georgia would turn against Native Americans.

Indeed, Indian Removal from eastern U. S. lands to west of the Mississippi River, was an on-again-off-again national policy. President Jefferson considered removal. [*John Ross and the Cherokee Indians* (1914) by Rachel Caroline Eaton at p. 21, cited by Wikipedia, *Cherokee Nation v. Georgia*].

President Monroe disfavored removal. [Eaton at p. 22]. John Ross was the principal Chief of the Cherokee Nation. In 1823, the U. S. Congress appropriated $30,000 towards stripping the Cherokee of tribal lands. [Eaton, at p.39]. Ross saw no hope in further entreaty to President Andrew Jackson, a former Indian fighter. Ross appealed without success to Senators Henry Clay and Daniel Webster, and Representative Davy Crockett. In 1830, Congress passed the *Indian Removal Act*, authorizing displacement of the Cherokee Nation to the Oklahoma Territory.

What is surprising is that Chief Justice John Marshall could not find a way to grant the Cherokee Nation relief. *Cherokee Nation v. Georgia*, 30 U.S. 1 (1831).

> "If Courts were permitted to indulge their sympathies, a case better calculated to excite them can scarcely be imagined. A people once numerous, powerful, and truly independent, found by our ancestors in the quiet and uncontrolled possession of an ample domain, gradually sinking beneath our superior policy, our arts and our arms, have yielded their land by successive treaties, *each of which contains a solemn guarantee of the residue, until* they retain no more of their formerly extensive territory than is deemed necessary to their comfortable existence." 30 U.S. at p. 15 (italics added).

> "Though the Indians are acknowledged to have an unquestionable, and heretofore unquestioned right to the lands they occupy, until that right shall be extinguished by a

voluntary cession to our government, yet it may well be doubted whether those tribes which reside within the acknowledged boundaries of the United States can, with strict accuracy, be denominated foreign nations. They may, more correctly, perhaps, be denominated, domestic dependent nations. They occupy a territory to which we assert title independent of their will, which must take effect in point of possession when their right of possession ceases. Meanwhile they are in s state of pupilage. Their relation to the United States resembles that of a ward to his guardian." 30 U.S. 17.

"This Court has bestowed is best attention on this [jurisdiction] question, and, after mature deliberation, the majority is of the opinion that an Indian tribe or nation within the United States is not a foreign state in the sense of the Constitution, and cannot maintain an action in the Courts of the United States," 30 U.S. at p. 20. "If it be true that the Cherokee Nation have rights, this is not the tribunal in which those rights are to be asserted. If it be true that wrongs have been inflicted, and that still greater are to be apprehended, this is not the tribunal which can redress the past or prevent the future."

What Chief Justice Marshall was saying in 1831 was that Native Americans could surrender their lands by treaty with the U.S., and the treaties would all solemnly guarantee Indians' right to remaining lands, but that the U. S. Supreme Court would not enforce rights granted to Indians in those treaties. Marshall feared that President Andrew Jackson would ignore any relief the Court granted to the Cherokee Nation.

By 1832 Marshall's conscience was stirring. *Worcester v. Georgia*, 31 U.S. 515, vacated the conviction of Samuel Worcester and sentence to four years at hard labor, and declared unconstitutional the Georgia criminal law that made it a crime for non-native Americans to be on Indian lands without a state license and oath to support Georgia's Constitution and laws. Worcester was a member of a group of missionaries living on Cherokee land. Marshall vacated Worcester's conviction, ruling that the State of Georgia had no jurisdiction over Indian Territory.

"The Cherokee nation, then, is a distinct community, occupying its own territory, with boundaries accurately described, in which the laws of Georgia can have no force, and which the citizens of Georgia have no right to enter but with the assent of the Cherokees themselves, or in conformity with treaties and with the acts of Congress. The whole intercourse between the United States and this [Cherokee] nation is by our Constitution and laws, vested in the Government of the United States." *Worcester v. Georgia*, 31 U.S. at p. 520.

In dicta, Marshall elaborated on the obligations of the U. S. government to Indian Tribes. President Jackson is quoted as saying that Marshall wrote the opinion, let him enforce it.

Georgia released Samuel Worcester upon assurance that he would stay out of Indian Lands. The state proceeded to expropriate lands of the Cherokee Nation, who pursuant to the Indian Removal Act, traveled the *Trail of Tears* to the Oklahoma Territory, with thousands of Cherokee dying in the migration.

Sarah Palin's concerns about Barack Obama "palling around with terrorists" like former Weatherman Bill Ayers. Michael Cooper, *Palin, On Offensive, Attacks Obama's Ties to '60s Radical*, New York Times, 10/408; Wikipedia, Barack Obama Presidential Campaign2008, The Truth about Barack Obama and William Ayers.

Huddled Masses. Written by Emma Lazarus, the Poem, The New Colossus, is inscribed on a plaque at the base of the Statue of Liberty. Here is the last part.

> Give me your tired, your poor,
> Your huddled masses yearning to breathe free,
> The wretched refuse of your teeming shore.
> Send these, the homeless, termpest-tost to me,
> I lift my lamp beside the golden door!

Chapter 5, Contract On America

Newt Gingrich and Richard Armey released the Contract With America during the 1994 election campaign. The Contract adopted ideas promoted by the Heritage Foundation and President Ronald Reagan. Jeffrey Gayner 10/12/95, *The Contract With America: Implementing New Ideas in the U.S.*, Heritage

Foundation. The Contract promised a balanced budget, smaller government, lower taxes, welfare reform and tort reform. The Cato Institute reported that the combined budgets of programs the Contract promised to eliminate increased by thirteen percent. Edward H. Crane, 11/13/2000, *On My Mind, GOP Pussycats*, Forbes magazine, Cato Institute. cf. Wikipedia, *Contract With America*.

Republicans voted Newt Gingrich out as House Speaker in January 1999, and he left congress to make some money. Dick Armey left Congress in 2002 to make more money.

The Gerrymander. The way politicians hold on to their seats is to draw the voting district lines to give them an unfair advantage. After the decennial census in 2010, Republicans controlled more state legislatures than did Democrats. State legislatures carved out election districts to give Republicans a majority in more districts and democrats a super majority in other districts. A state could elect a Democratic Governor, and, at the same time, have Republican control in the state legislature and in the U. S. House of Representatives. Gerrymandering goes back to Elbridge Gerry, Governor of Massachusetts in 1812.

Conventional wisdom is that Republicans will hold control of the U.S. House in 2014. The trend, however, started back for the Democrats in 2012. Democrats received a million more votes than Republicans received in congressional districts in U.S. House elections in 2012.

The composition of the House is supposed to represent the will of the people. Gerrymandering allows politicians to override the will of the people. Republican State Leadership Committee admits it won by gerrymandering blue state election districts. *ThinkProgress*, 1/17/13, *Republicans Brag They Won House Seats Because of Gerrymandering*, by Scott Keyes; *Huffington Post*, 7/29/14, *GOP REDMAP Memo Admits Gerrymandering To Thank For Congressional Election Success*, by Nick Wing.

U.S. House 2012. Democrats in Pennsylvania won half of the votes, but Republicans took three quarters of the House Seats. A majority of voters in North Carolina voted for Democrats, but Republicans took seventy percent of the seats. Voters chose Democrats over Republicans in Michigan, but Republicans took nine out of fourteen seats. Gerrymandering also allowed politicians to thwart the will of the people in Florida, Wisconsin, Ohio and Virginia. *Mother Jones*, 11/14/12. *Now That's What I call Gerrymandering!* by Adam Serwer, Jaeah Lee and Zaineb Mohammed.

When the voters realize in 2014 or 2016 that politicians are holding office through gerrymandering, and when voters consider Republican obstruction in Congress since 2011, voters likely will sweep Democrats back into the majority in the U.S. House.

Chapter 6, Groundhog Day.

Senator McCain could have been a positive force for good, as a member of the loyal opposition. McCain acts more like a sore loser after Obama's win in 2008. Obama may have made a mistake by not bringing McCain into his confidence early on in 2009. The GOP pledge that politics stops at the water's edge does not apply to the GOP lockstep opposition to all things Obama.

Chapter 7, Be Far Right Or Be Gone.

Partisanship and financial disparity is tearing the country apart. The Congress cannot function because the pull from each extreme keeps the majority away from the middle. If the battle was an honest dispute over policy, differences could resolve. The battle, however, is a struggle by the superrich to suppress everyone else. Since Government can levy taxes to raise funds to provide services, the wealthy want to cut government and eliminate government services.

To the extent that the upper one percent are successful, inevitably they will bring about their own downfall. If the Republicans take control of the U.S. Government in 2016, and implement Paul Ryan's Plan Forward, a wave of disenfranchised Americans will present their grievances. What we will see is a French Revolution, rebelling from the bottom up, without a Louis XVI. Mitt Romney, as a fluent French speaker, could play the role of Louis VXI.

America's strength was not isolated in the Rockefellers, Carnegies, Vanderbilts, Fords or Mellons. America became a great country because it had a middle class who could afford the American dream. In 1914, Henry Ford raised his workers' pay to $5.00 a day in the hope that each worker could afford to buy a Ford. The United States' economy is 2/3d's based upon consumer spending. With the U.S. middle class jettisoned by corporate greed in the race to the wage bottom, the recession of 2008-2010 is recovering in fits and starts.

Chapter 8, Liberate Kansas!

Fossil Fuels Lobby. "All over the USA, identikit bills and resolutions appear in State legislatures-all designed to suppress the US's growing renewable energy sector." Ecologist, May 27, 2014, article by Farron Cousins, Executive Editor of Trial Lawyer Magazine. Koch Brothers and Exxon-Mobile use *ALEC* to package proposed bills in identikit fashion for state legislatures to adopt, verbatim if possible.

Koch Brothers have increased to $3.6 million their advertising spending on Monica Wehby, candidate for the U. S. Senate from Oregon. *Koch Brothers Throw More Money*, Huffington Post, 7/25/14, updated 725/14, by Zach Carter. In addition to *Americans for* [Koch Brothers'] *Prosperity*, the Koch Brothers have a 501(c)(6) group headquartered in Virginia called *Freedom Partners* that is supporting Wehby against incumbent Jeff Merkely.

If *Freedom Partners* is not primarily a social welfare organization, its tax-exempt status is in question. *Freedom Partners* is a double blind cover for the top two percent to use to keep control of the government away from the bottom ninety eighty percent. Koch Brothers contribute to *Freedom Partners*, which funnels money to other front groups such as FreedomWorks.

In 2012, *Freedom Partners* distributed more than $250 million to other front groups, without disclosing the identity of its donors. The Koch Brothers Secret Bank, Politico, September 11, 2013, by Mike Allen and Jim Vendehei. According to the IRS, the types of organizations exempt under §501(c)(6) are Business Leagues, Chambers of Commerce, Real Estate Boards and Professional Football Leagues. IRS.gov. *Freedom Partners* does not qualify for tax exempt status.

Chapter 9, Nihilism & Emotional Instability.

Republicans have made a religion out of criticizing the federal government. Matt Kibbe is President and CEO of *FreedomWorks*, a 501(c)(4) group whose banner reads, *Government Fails. Freedom Works*. One of their issues is *Stop Eric Holders Paycheck*. Matt Kibbe paid former Majority Leader Dick Armey $8 million to step down as Chair of FreedomWorks in November 2012. *Inside the Dick Armey, FreedomWorks split*, Politico, 12/4/12, by Kenneth P. Vogel. In 2010 Armey and Kibbe wrote *Give Us Liberty: a Tea Party Manifesto.*

FreedomWorks staff worked on the project and FreedomWorks had the proceeds of sales. In 2012, Kibbe planned to write *Hostile Takeover: Resisting Centralized Government's Stranglehold on America.* Kibbe reportedly wanted to use FreedomWorks staff on the book, but keep the proceeds for himself. Armey reportedly stepped down because Kibbe asked him to lie staff work on Kibbe's book.

Chapter 10, GOP: Born to Protect Civil Rights

The GOP has strayed so far from its original mission that it should not be allowed to use the name, *Republican*. The post Civil War Amendments that abolished slavery (13th Amend.), defined citizenship (14th Amend.), and prohibited discrimination in voting based on race (15th Amend.), and the basic Civil Rights laws were enacted with Republican sponsorship from 1865 to 1876.

The Civil Rights Act of 1964 (making use of public facilities of restaurants, hotels and trains available to all) first became law in *1876*. In 1883, The U.S. Supreme Court held sections 1 and 2 of the Civil Rights Act of 1876 unconstitutional. Civil Rights would go to the back burner for ninety years. The Supreme Court ruled that the 14th Amendment prohibited discrimination by states and did not apply to private individuals or businesses.

Chapter 11, Rape of Religious Freedom.

Jerry Falwell.

"If Chief Justice Warren and his associates had known God's word and had desired to do God's will, I am quite content that the 1954 decision would never had been made. The facilities would be separate. When God has drawn a line of distinction, we should not attempt to cross that line."

Jerry Falwell, quoted in the Nation, May 28, 2007. *See* Wikipedia, Jerry Falwell.

Falwell founded Liberty University, the largest private university in the U.S. It is telling that Senator John McCain, the independent-minded maverick, gave the commencement address at Liberty University in May 2006. McCain previously branded Falwell an agent of intolerance.

Planned Parenthood of Southeast Pennsylvania v. Casey, 505 U.S. 833 (1992).

Chapter 12, Can Money Buy Political Power?

Paralysis in Congress demonstrates the political power of the Koch Brothers and casino magnate Sheldon Adelson. George W. Bush's election was a disaster for the nation. Bush allowed the neoconservatives, led by Dick Cheney, Donald Rumsfeld and Paul Wolfowitz, to lead us into a quagmire in Iraq. Bush nominated Samuel Alioto and John Roberts to the Supreme Court.

Recent Supreme Court decisions (*Citizens United v. FEC, McCutcheon v. FEC*) eviscerated limitations on campaign funding, and (*Shelby County, Alabama, v. Holder*) promoted discrimination by overturning the pre-clearance requirements for Southern States to obtain Justice Department approval for changes to voting qualifications, places and conditions.

Sharron Angle. Bob Cashell, Mayor of Reno, dismissed Sharron as an ultra right winger. I will support Reid, Bob Cashell, Video, KRNV-DT, June 9, 2010.

Chapter 15, Danger From the Right.

The quote by Quintus, about a conquered people, is from the film, *Gladiator*.

###

Other Books by Paul Covell

May be ordered from e-tailers at Smash-words.com and as a pocketbook from create-space.com

1. *G.O.P. War on U.S.*, createspace 3955908

2. *The Hail Mary* [Romney's 2012 run for president], createspace 3989582

3. *D'Souza's Delusion*, createspace 4010070

_____

###